Praise for HUNDREDS OF HEADS™ *Survival Guides:*

"Hundreds of Heads is an innovative publishing house... Its entertaining and informative 'How To Survive ...' series takes a different approach to offering advice. Thousands of people around the nation were asked for their firsthand experiences and real-life tips in six of life's arenas. Think 'Chicken Soup' meets 'Zagats,' says a press release, and rightfully so."

—ALLEN O. PIERLEONI, "BETWEEN THE LINES," THE SACRAMENTO BEE

"A concept that will be... a huge seller and a great help to people. I firmly believe that today's readers want sound bytes of information, not tomes. Your series will most definitely be the next 'Chicken Soup.'"

—CYNTHIA BRIAN
TV/RADIO PERSONALITY, BEST SELLING AUTHOR: CHICKEN SOUP FOR THE GARDENER'S SOUL; BE THE STAR YOU ARE!; THE BUSINESS OF SHOW BUSINESS

"Move over, 'Dummies'... Can that 'Chicken Soup!' Hundreds of Heads are on the march to your local bookstore!"

—ELIZABETH HOPKINS,
KFNX (PHOENIX) RADIO HOST, THINKING OUTSIDE THE BOX

Praise for other titles in the HUNDREDS OF HEADS™ *Survival Guide series:*

HOW TO LOSE 9,000 LBS. (OR LESS)

"Informative and entertaining... a must-read if you have ever struggled with the delicate 'D' word."

—ZORA ANDRICH
REALITY SHOW CONTESTANT

"For all of those people who say they've 'been there, done that' when it comes to dieting—this book actually goes there and does that, to show us how to be successful in our own quest for permanent weight loss."

—SUSIE GALVEZ
BEAUTY INDUSTRY EXPERT AND AUTHOR; LOST 120 LBS.

HOW TO SURVIVE YOUR TEENAGER

"Parents of teens and parents of kids approaching those years will find wisdom on each page...provides insight, humor, and empathy..."
—FOREWORD MAGAZINE, *JULY/AUGUST 2005*

"These anecdotes, written by people who have been there, hit the nail on the head! Some you'll recognize as wonderful suggestions or insightful descriptions of true-life experiences. Others will help you recognize traps to avoid. This book tells it like it is."
—*STEVEN PERLOW, PH.D.*
CLINICAL PSYCHOLOGIST, ATLANTA, GEORGIA

"With warmth, humor and 'I've been there' compassion, editors Gluck and Rosenfeld have turned the ordinary experiences and struggles of parents into bits of compact wisdom that are easy to pick up and use straightaway. I especially liked this book's many examples of how to survive (and even thrive) while living under the same roof as your teen."
—*JACLYNN MORRIS, M.ED.*
CO-AUTHOR OF I'M RIGHT. YOU'RE WRONG. NOW WHAT? AND FROM ME TO YOU

HOW TO SURVIVE YOUR FRESHMAN YEAR

"This book proves that all of us are smarter than one of us."
—*JOHN KATZMAN*
FOUNDER AND CEO, PRINCETON REVIEW

"Voted in the Top 40 Young Adults books."
—*PENNSYLVANIA SCHOOL LIBRARIANS ASSOCIATION*

"This cool new book...helps new college students get a head start on having a great time and making the most of this new and exciting experience."
—*COLLEGE OUTLOOK*

"This book is right on the money. I wish I had this before I started college."
—*KATIE LEVITT*
SENIOR, GEORGE WASHINGTON UNIVERSITY

HOW TO SURVIVE DATING

"Rated one of the Top 10 Dating Books."
—ABOUT.COM

"Invaluable advice... If I had read this book before I made my movie, it would have been only *10 Dates*."
—MYLES BERKOWITZ, FILMMAKER. WROTE, DIRECTED AND WENT OUT ON 20 DATES FOR FOX SEARCHLIGHT

"Great, varied advice, in capsule form, from the people who should know—those who've dated and lived to tell the tale."
—SALON.COM

"Hilarious!"
—TEENA JONES
THE TEENA JONES SHOW, *KMSR-AM (DALLAS)*

HOW TO SURVIVE A MOVE

"As a realtor, I see the gamut of moving challenges. This book is great - covering everything from a 'heads-up' on the travails of moving to suggested solutions for the problems. AND... it's a great read!"
—JEANNE MOELLENDICK, *RE/MAX SPECIALISTS, JACKSONVILLE, FLORIDA*

"How to Survive A Move is full of common sense ideas and moving experiences from every-day people. I have been in the moving industry for 22 years and I was surprised at all the new ideas I learned from your book!"
—FRED WALLACE, PRESIDENT, ONE BIG MAN & ONE BIG TRUCK MOVING COMPANY

"A good resource book for do-it-yourself movers to learn some of the best tips in making a move easier."
—JOANNE FRIED, U-HAUL INTERNATIONAL, INC.

HOW TO SURVIVE YOUR MARRIAGE

"I love this book!"
—Donna Britt, Host, Lifetime Radio

"Reader-friendly and packed full of good advice. They should hand this out at the marriage license counter!"
—Bob Nachshin, Celebrity Divorce Attorney and Co-Author of I do, You do . . . But Just Sign Here

"Full of honest advice from newlyweds and longtime couples. This book answers the question—'How do other people do it?'"
—Ellen Sabin, M.P.H., M.P.A., Executive Director, Equality in Marriage Institute

HOW TO SURVIVE YOUR BABY'S FIRST YEAR

"What to read when you're reading the other baby books. The perfect companion for your first-year baby experience."
—Susan Reingold, M.A., Educator

"*How to Survive Your Baby's First Year*...offers tried-and-true methods of baby care and plenty of insight to the most fretted about parenting topics..."
—Bookviews

"Full of real-life ideas and tips. If you love superb resource books for being the best parent you can be, you'll love *How to Survive Your Baby's First Year.*"
—Erin Brwon Conroy, M.A.
Author, Columnist, Mother of Twelve, and Creator of Totallyfitmom.com

"The Hundreds of Heads folks have done it again! Literally hundreds of moms and dads from all over offer their nuggets of wisdom—some sweet, some funny, all smart—on giving birth, coming home and bringing up baby."
—Andrea Sarvady
Author of Baby Gami

How
to Survive
the Real
World

WARNING:

This guide contains differing opinions. Hundreds of heads will not always agree. Advice taken in combination may cause unwanted side effects. Use your head when selecting advice.

How

Life after College
Graduation

to Survive
the Real
World

ANDREA SYRTASH, SPECIAL EDITOR

Hundreds of Heads Books, LLC

ATLANTA

Illustrations © 2006 by Image Club
Cover photograph by PictureQuest
Cover and book design by Elizabeth Johnsboen

Library of Congress Cataloging-in-Publication Data

How to survive the real world : life after college graduation / Andrea Syrtash, special editor.
    p. cm.
  ISBN-13: 978-1-933512-03-7
  ISBN-10: 1-933512-03-2
1. Life skills--United States. 2. College graduates--United States--Life skills guides.
3. School-to-work transition--United States. I. Syrtash, Andrea.
  HQ2039.U6H675 2006
  646.70084'2--dc22
                              2005037773

See page 190 for credits and permissions.

HUNDREDS OF HEADS® books are available at special discounts when purchased in bulk for premiums or institutional or educational use. Excerpts and custom editions can be created for specific uses. For more information, please e-mail sales@hundredsofheads.com or write to:

HUNDREDS OF HEADS BOOKS, LLC
#230
2221 Peachtree Road, Suite D
Atlanta, Georgia 30309

ISBN-10: 1-933512-03-2
ISBN-13: 978-1933512-03-7

Printed in U.S.A.
10 9 8 7 6 5 4 3 2 1

CONTENTS

Introduction

S o, when exactly *do* you become an adult? Under the laws in the United States, you are considered an adult at the age of 18—at least, if you want to join the military or vote. If you want to have a drink, you (legally) have to be 21.

Coming-of-age rituals exist all over the world in religious and secular forms. In Australia and New Zealand, it's common to throw a 21st birthday party to celebrate adulthood. And in Korea, the Confucian rite of passage, called Gwallye, is held for girls and boys between the ages of 15 and 20.

And then there is your college graduation, that rite of passage into so-called adulthood, when you presumably leave behind your schooling and set off to conquer your dreams in the so-called real world. Also, you have to pay your own bills. As a reader of this book, we're guessing you're at this point in your life and you're curious about how the years ahead might unfold. You've come to the right place.

In *How to Survive the Real World: Life After College Graduation*, we've collected hundreds of stories from real-world survivors across the country. The result: an entertaining and helpful guide filled with anecdotes and advice on the pressing issues that you are facing. To live close to your parents or in a city far away? To travel abroad for a year or settle into a career. What's the best way to find a job? What are proven ways to impress your new boss? What are some tips for paying off school debt and staying out of financial trouble? How best to stay in touch with old friends while making new ones? At your first adult party, what sort of food and drink do you serve? How do you stay spiritually and physically healthy? And, perhaps most important, where's a good place to find someone to date?

We all have different concerns and values. Some of us strive for a meaningful life in which we are spiritually centered and feel deeply connected to our community. Some of us live for fun and adventure, enjoying our singlehood and all of the perks of living in a big city. Whatever you're seeking, you'll find answers here, from people who have already "been there, done that."

At Hundreds of Heads Books, we believe that if two heads are better than one, how awesome must hundreds of heads be? With that in mind, consider this book as you would hundreds of wise mentors who are willing to help you through this challenging stage of personal growth.

Most of all, take time to explore and enjoy this new chapter of life. The adventure is just beginning …

ANDREA SYRTASH

Adult Life: What's That?

It might not get the attention of a midlife crisis, but the age when you leave behind your schooling and enter the real world is certainly rife with anxiety. And where there is a personal crisis, there are meaning-of-life questions: Are you really an adult now? Will you ever feel like an adult? What is an adult? What are you going to do with your life? What is the meaning of life? Does it have good benefits? More than two million college grads consider these questions every year. As you take your first steps into adulthood, we provide answers and personal stories.

I WAS STUNNED when I finished college. I literally sat around, staring ahead of me, saying, "What am I going to do?!"

—A.C.
TORONTO, ONTARIO, CANADA

I NEVER WANTED TO LEAVE COLLEGE. I WANTED TO BE A STUDENT FOREVER.

—LEANNE
ATLANTA, GEORGIA

HEADLINES
Best Advice and Top Tips

- Finding your way in the world takes time—be patient.
- The first step to becoming an adult is to realize your parents will no longer bail you out of everything.
- When you're in your 20s it's the perfect time to think about what you want out of life and what's important to you.
- Being 21 may make you legally an adult, but maturity comes much later.
- Take your time—it's OK if you don't have a marriage, a house, a career, and kids by the time you're 25.

ATTENTION BUSINESS GRADS

New college grads spend more than $40 billion a year getting equipped for adult life.

UPON GRADUATING COLLEGE, I employed a reliable, time-honored strategy: stalling. I convinced my financial benefactors—my parents—to support my indolent lifestyle for a few extra years by floating ambitious career plans without making too much headway. This approach works. Irresponsibility, bad behavior, and fun should not end with college. You do have to work and pay back loans, but at the same time you can screw up, try a few different things and find out what works best for you. If you are 25, without a marriage, career, mortgage, and kids, that's just fine. It is probably all for the better.

—A.F.
NEW YORK, NEW YORK

ADULT LIFE MEANS THAT THERE IS NO ONE there to wake you up in the morning if you oversleep, no one there to make sure you eat right, no one there to remind you to take your medication, and no one there to turn off the television if you leave it on when you go to sleep. Adult life means you have to do for yourself.

—*KELLEY FREID*
POLAND, OHIO

• • • • • • • •

" Your 20s are this golden period of opportunity; don't waste it. Think hard about what you might regret. What is really important to you? Money? Love? Security? Adventure? It's different things for different people. "

—*GRACE*
CHAPEL HILL, NORTH CAROLINA

• • • • • • • •

WE'RE INUNDATED WITH HOLLYWOOD images about how our first love, our first job, and our life will look as adults. In a way, we're set up to reach for things that may not be realistic. Finding your way takes time, and it helps to know others feel this way, too.

—*J.B.*
TRURO, NOVA SCOTIA, CANADA

NEED A LIFE COACH?

Life coaching: Used by a growing number of psychologists to aid clients with transitions in their personal life, and in the process of self-actualization. Life coaching draws from a number of disciplines, including sociology, psychology, career counseling, and other types of counseling. The coach, or counselor, applies mentoring, values assessment, behavior modification, behavior modeling, goal setting, and other techniques in assisting clients.

I first knew I was an adult when I asked someone to turn the music down.

—*Raquel*
San Francisco,
California

I LOST A LOT OF SLEEP AFTER GRADUATION and had a few panic attacks. Men and women in my generation feel a great amount of pressure to succeed at a young age. It is more important to travel, continue school (i.e., graduate school, if possible), find yourself, and feel happy and strong on your own before entering the workforce. The real world will always be waiting, so make sure that you see and experience everything before you are tied down to a certain amount of vacation days and time constraints.

—*Steph Mathews*
St. Louis, Missouri

. . . .

I STILL DON'T FEEL LIKE MY OWN PERSON. At 22 years old, I feel like I borrowed bits of other people's personalities. I don't know if that makes sense, but I just don't really understand who I am yet. But I understand others and what I like about them, so I adopt those traits. Maybe this is what it's all about. Hopefully I will become more than just the cool things about other people as I get older.

—*Jessica*
Seattle, Washington

MY PARENTS FUNDED EVERYTHING IN COLLEGE.
Maybe I was spoiled. But there's none of that in
the "real world." You're not working a part-time
job so you have some bar money on the weekends. You're working full time so you can pay
rent, cable, phone, and electricity bills; you work
to live. If you don't do your laundry, you can't put
on dirty clothes and stroll to class. You have to
have ironed clothes for client meetings. In the
"real world," you're more accountable for all of
your actions, and you're truly independent.

> —JIM
> HOBOKEN, NEW JERSEY

I'M 31 YEARS OLD and still don't feel like an adult.
On the airplane yesterday I saw a man who
looked like he was born an adult. He was with his
wife and young kids, and he was probably not
much older than I am. He had an adult watch,
adult clothes. Adults seem to compartmentalize
their lives in neat sections: job, family, finances,
and so on. I'm still trying to prepare myself for
this.

> —MICHAEL ALBERT PAOLI
> TORONTO, ONTARIO, CANADA

I FELT LIKE A GROWN-UP WHEN I realized that I and
my space—the space I take up on this earth—are
just as important as anyone else and the space
they take up. Once you realize that, you can
stand there and not be intimidated by anybody
else. That's when I started feeling like an adult.

> —JOEY
> CAPE COD, MASSACHUSETTS

I recall Dean
Wormer's
advice from
Animal House:
"Fat, drunk
and stupid is
no way to go
through life,
son."

> —ANONYMOUS
> GENEVA, OHIO

YOU'RE FREE! CELEBRATING YOUR GRADUATION

I WENT SKINNY-DIPPING WITH THREE FRIENDS at Table Rock Lake—totally impromptu and totally awesome. It was the most invigorating, timeless afternoon I have ever experienced. I felt so free and unguarded. It's like shedding the bathing suit also shed my insecurities, my need for self-preservation. It sounds corny, but it's totally true. Everyone should do this at least once in his or her life. But look out, because it can become addictive!

—*ANGELA WILSON*
SPRINGFIELD, MISSOURI

FORGET A PARTY. Get the hell out of town (on your parents' dime) and enjoy every last bit of irresponsible behavior you can possibly stand. I went to Aruba for a week after I graduated and absorbed every last second of the comforts of the family benefit plan.

—*KRISTI KAMERMAN*
BATON ROUGE, LOUISIANA

MY MOM AND I WENT TO A DUDE RANCH IN COLORADO for a week and a half to celebrate my graduation. I love horses, and it was something I had always wanted to do. It was great because we got to spend some quality time together. She told me how proud she was of me for getting my degree. It was really special. I'm glad that I had the opportunity to celebrate with my mom, especially now that I'm starting my career and don't have as much free time.

—*JACKIE MOORE*
OZARK, MISSOURI

I CELEBRATED ONE NIGHT AT OUR FAVORITE COLLEGE BAR with my friends and family, then woke up the next morning and started my job as a meat cutter at a barbecue joint to pay the bills until I found a "real job." I got 50 cents more an hour than anyone else because I was the only meat cutter with a college degree.

—JAMES RINEY
FORT WORTH, TEXAS

• • • • • • • •

THE DAY AFTER MY GRADUATION, my mom and I went out and I bought a brand-new Honda Civic. There were only six miles on that baby, and that was after my test drive. I felt like I was signing my life away.

—K.R.
BELLEVILLE, ILLINOIS

• • • • • • • •

GRADUATION FROM COLLEGE WAS one of the most surreal times of my life. Be sure to make time for everyone that meant something to you during that magical time of your undergrad. Eat at all your favorite places. Have a drink at your favorite bar. Spend time at the fountain where you and your roommate would eat pints of ice cream and talk about boys. Celebrate all of your recent successes and all those that are waiting ahead of you. Even if you can't get everyone together at once, figure out a way to see them. You never know when you'll see them again.

—ERIN HUDAK
AUSTIN, TEXAS

WHEN I FIRST HIT THE ADULT AGE OF **21,** it meant I was old enough to do adult things. I could live where I wanted and drink what I wanted. Being a mature adult came a lot later, and proved to be a learn-as-you-go process. I wanted people to take me seriously, and it took a lot of falling down. There was still a part of me that wanted to be young and carefree. It took a lot of practice.

—CHRISTOPHER
HAVERTOWN, PENNSYLVANIA

. . . .

"A few years ago the check-out guy at the supermarket called me 'Ma'am,' and I knew that must mean I'm an adult. I wanted to slap him and say, 'What happened to 'Miss'?'"

—RANAI
SAN FRANCISCO, CALIFORNIA

. . . .

DO WHAT MAKES YOU HAPPY. I spent five years working for our family business. I realized I was on my way to becoming an adult just recently, when I told my family that I wanted to work elsewhere. I just landed my first job on my own, doing something totally different. I love my family, but I want to make it on my own.

—TAWNY WHITE
SPRINGFIELD, MISSOURI

THE GOOD, THE BAD, AND THE UGLY AFTER COLLEGE

The good is that you're young, with a degree, and a sexy body. The bad is that it's all you have. You're fabulous but broke; you're educated but at a mind-numbing, entry-level job; and you have rent out the wazoo. The ugly is that this nightmare will continue for a few more years. When do I get the Cosmo life? When do I get my hot job so that I can afford to buy the gold strappy Dolce & Gabbana shoes that I desire? How much longer do I have to wait until I discover my passion in life?

We need to take it one day at a time. We need to tell ourselves it's OK. But even more important, we need to believe it. In due time things will work out. It may not be today, tomorrow, or next year, but with enough gumption it will happen. The amazing job, the prestige, the shoes, the loves—we just need to get through these cloudy days of being 20-something.

—J.
WASHINGTON, D.C.

WHAT ARE YOU?

Main entry: adult
Function: noun
1: one that has arrived at full development or maturity especially in size, strength, or intellectual capacity
2: a human male or female after a specific age (as 18 or 21)

BEING AN ADULT MEANS that when you create a problem for yourself, you have to solve it yourself. It's the point in your life where you can't turn to Mom and Dad to bail you out. It means being personally responsible for yourself and your actions. If you find yourself still looking around for someone else to clean up things that you did wrong, you are not yet an adult.

—*SUZANNE EDENHART*
WILLIAMSTOWN, KENTUCKY

• • • • • • • •

THERE HAVE BEEN A NUMBER of those moments in my life when I have realized I'm an adult, but none of them have ever really stuck. I feel grown-up in the moment, but I go back to feeling like my same dorky self when the moment has passed. This usually occurs when something significant happens: taking my first salaried job, having my babies, buying a house. During these rites of passage, I usually take a moment and acknowledge a (fleeting) sense of "adultness"; the rest of the time, I still feel 16.

—*ELENA*
CHICAGO, ILLINOIS

• • • • • • • •

IF YOU STOP ASKING THE QUESTION "What should I do with my life?" life will hold little meaning, and your talents could be left undiscovered. I face this question every day. No matter how "successful" I have become or how comfortable I feel with my current situation—job or no job, relationship or not—I find myself asking questions: What is my purpose? Why am I here? So far, I haven't been able to answer. But the fact that I have asked in the first place is progress in itself.

—*JERALYN*
AUSTIN, TEXAS

I FIRST FELT LIKE AN ADULT when I was 28 and got my first haircut in a salon. When I was growing up, we never had any money, so my mother cut my hair herself. When my older sister became a beautician, she always did our hair. But when I was 28 and I got my tax return back, I decided I wanted to have my hair cut in a salon. I was horrified at the price I paid, but I loved it so much, and it made me feel so much better about myself. Now that's my one indulgence.

—*BETH*
SHAKOPEE, MINNESOTA

· · · · · · · ·

FOR THE PAST FEW YEARS since graduating college, I haven't been as social. I wanted to figure out what was important to me by figuring it out on my own, not by joining a larger community and figuring it out by what others deemed to be important. This was my intuition, and I followed it. Instead of trying A, B, and C, I opted for X, Y, Z. Be open to listening to your instincts; they come from a deep place. Postcollege is a time of change, and it's very personal.

—*NICHOLAS WEISS*
SAN FRANCISCO, CALIFORNIA

· · · · · · · ·

I'M STILL WAITING TO FEEL LIKE AN ADULT. The closest I came was when I bought my first new car. I negotiated with the car dealer by myself.

—*JULIANA GOODWIN*
SPRINGFIELD, MISSOURI

· · · · · · · ·

THERE WAS CERTAINLY A POINT when I thought, "Oh, shit. My parents are not going to bail me out of this anymore." It is a powerful feeling.

—*J.G.*
CHAPEL HILL, NORTH CAROLINA

You only live once. Go with the flow ... or paddle like hell.

—*JOE*
BOSTON
MASSACHUSETTS

I don't go out during the week anymore, but my weekends are just the same: pure debauchery.

—JIM
  HOBOKEN, NEW
  JERSEY

DON'T GROW OLD TOO FAST by worrying prematurely about a career, family, and so on. The opportunity for trying out all kinds of work, even experimenting with not working at all (spare change, food stamps, selling all your belongings and living in the woods) is not to be missed. Follow your whims: pump gas, preach the apocalypse, worship the devil, volunteer in a nursing home, and get to know the joys and regrets of people at the other end of the road. It's impossible to screw up your life so much at this stage that it can't be repaired with a little dedication and hard work somewhere down the line. One of the most freeing verses I've ever heard was Bob Dylan's: "It's alright, Ma: it's life and life only."

—JOE
  BOSTON, MASSACHUSETTS

· · · · · · · ·

I REALIZED I WAS AN ADULT when I chaperoned my first high school dance. It was shocking. I mean, when did I become a grown-up? It just snuck up on me.

—ANDREA FREYGANG
  DEERFIELD BEACH, FLORIDA

· · · · · · · ·

I KNEW I WAS AN ADULT when others started to view me as one. Example: Once I stayed out way too late and did something I probably shouldn't have been doing. The next day I got a call from a friend and I told him what I did. He said, "Hey man, you're grown up now. You've got a real job. You can't act like that anymore."

—BRANDON
  DALLAS, TEXAS

ADULT LIFE TO ME: NO MORE COLLEGE BREAKS!
This meant no more spring break and no more month-long Christmas breaks. This was the hardest part for me.

—MICAH BARBER
SILVERTON, TEXAS

• • • • • • • •

I KNEW I WAS AN ADULT when I filled out the tax forms for my new job and didn't claim dependency on my father. Oh, and that first round of utility bills did it too.

—LACEY CONNELLY
CHICAGO, ILLINOIS

• • • • • • • •

ADULT LIFE MEANS PAYING FOR EVERYTHING yourself, not being able to blame others for your mistakes, gaining weight, and having to move heavy objects on your own.

—ELIZABETH
PHILADELPHIA, PENNSYLVANIA

• • • • • • • •

MOVING AWAY TO COLLEGE is much different than moving to a new city once you graduate. When you're still in college, you might be far from home, like I was, but you're still connected to your family—through money, through visits, through the way you are seen in your parents' eyes. Out of college, I moved away to a big city, and that's when I finally cut the apron strings and did whatever I wanted. It was freeing and frightening at the same time.

—MICHELE
HOLLY, MICHIGAN

WHEN DID I KNOW I WAS AN ADULT? I had been out of college for about a year, lost my job, and was about to get kicked out of my apartment because I was a month late with the rent. I went home to talk to my dad about it, subconsciously thinking he'd say I could move back home if it came down to it. But he told me the exact opposite. Without saying it in so many words, he told me that I'd have to find a way to get through it on my own. I knew then that I was welcome to visit, but that my days living there were over.

—*CAM THORNTON*
JAMESTOWN, NEW YORK

Oh, The Places You'll Go! On Traveling & Settling

For many graduates of past generations, the question of where to live was a nonissue. Most people lived near family, often in the cities in which they grew up. Today, it's as if there's been a travel-agent wakeup call to grads: You are not tied down; it's time to explore. Recent U.S. college graduates are traveling more than ever before: Some to see new sights on a long weekend, some to experience life on the road for months at a time, others to settle in the U.S. city of their dreams, and still others to work in international destinations. Where will you go? Where will you settle? And what kind of shelter will you have when you get there? Read on to find out about the adventures of others who went before you.

A NEW PLACE, A GREAT JOB and fun new people … it doesn't get much better than that!

—*J. KYLE KISER*
SCOTTSDALE, ARIZONA

DON'T BE AFRAID TO EXPLORE THE WORLD!

—*M.B.*
WEEHAWKEN, NEW JERSEY

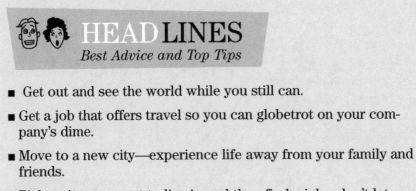

HEAD LINES
Best Advice and Top Tips

- Get out and see the world while you still can.
- Get a job that offers travel so you can globetrot on your company's dime.
- Move to a new city—experience life away from your family and friends.
- Pick a city you want to live in and then find a job—don't let work dictate where you live.
- Don't move someplace just because you're in love—unless you think you'll be happy there even if the relationship ends.

IT'S A BIG WORLD; GET OUT THERE AND SEE IT. My pet peeve is with people who spend all that time and money getting a college education and then limit themselves in where they can work and live by wanting to stay close to home. What a bunch of nonsense. If you are afraid to move too far away from Mommy, then you are never going to amount to anything. Do a nationwide job search and just go. My first job was in upstate Montana. I had never been to that part of the world in my life. It was so beautiful up there. And cold. But it forced me to act and think for myself because I was thousands of miles from my parents. It really caused me to grow up much faster than I would have had I stayed close to home.

—*CANDACE MISTELLI*
BOARDMAN, OHIO

MY TRAVEL EXCURSIONS so far have mostly involved breathtaking drives along the country's interstate system, cuisine at the nation's finest convenience stores and fast-food outlets, and luxurious stays at the Super 8 Motel's most exotic franchises. Weekends in the Caribbean are still just something I see footage of on the E! network.

—*JESSE AMMERMAN*
CHICAGO, ILLINOIS

* * * * * * * *

" I've always lived downtown. I *love* the atmosphere. Late at night when you wake up and look out, it's exciting and electrifying, yet peaceful at the same time. Plus, do you *know* how many hotties hang out there? "

—*RICH*
ANN ARBOR, MICHIGAN

* * * * * * * *

I LOVE VEGAS. I LIKE FANCY HOTELS. I like the nice restaurants, the shows, the entertainment opportunities. And the women are gorgeous! I don't make a lot of money, but I try to budget nearly every dollar I spend. That includes meals, souvenirs, lodging, gas. I plan way in advance.

—*R.S.*
SPRINGFIELD, MISSOURI

IT'S A GOOD EXPERIENCE FOR EVERYONE to have to adapt to a new place. When I graduated college, I went to Japan to teach English. I thought it would be a good move professionally, but looking back now, the biggest growth occurred personally. I learned a lot about myself by being in a different culture. It's like that old Zen expression, "If you don't bend, you'll break."

—*DARCY BELANGER*
SHERWOOD PARK, ALBERTA, CANADA

. . . .

" Pay the little bit extra to live in an area of town that you enjoy. I have a friend who lives 30-plus minutes outside the city in an apartment her parents own, for free. And she's miserable. "

—*ADAM SHALABY*
TORONTO, ONTARIO, CANADA

. . . .

WHEN I GRADUATED COLLEGE, I drove across the country with this boy I hardly knew. I took my graduation money and blew it. I had a wonderful time. It makes my hair stand up to think of some of the situations I got into. But I did the right thing up until then: I went straight from high school to college; I got good grades. I needed that time to find out who I was.

—*LAUREN*
CHAPEL HILL, NORTH CAROLINA

IN THE PAST, VACATION MEANT paying for transportation to a place where I knew someone. This way lodging was always free, and I got to see old friends. Now that I've been out of school for four years, I can finally afford to take a real vacation, to a city where I don't know anyone, and stay in a hotel. I can't afford a luxury vacation and have to take the time to search online to find the best deals, but it still feels very grown-up.

—M.B.
WEEHAWKEN, NEW JERSEY

SEEK ADVENTURE NOW. As soon as I graduated, I climbed Mount Popocatepetl in Mexico and Mount Washington in New Hampshire. They were both very challenging and both very different, but I summited both of them. I'm glad I did it before falling into a career. I'd love to go to Mount Everest sometime, but how do you tell your boss you need a month off work to go climb a big hill?

—ALISHA HIPWELL
FRANKFORT, KENTUCKY

10 MOST EXPENSIVE CITIES IN THE WORLD

1. Tokyo, Japan
2. Osaka, Japan
3. London, England
4. Moscow, Russia
5. Seoul, South Korea
6. Geneva, Switzerland
7. Zurich, Switzerland
8. Copenhagen, Denmark
9. Hong Kong, China
10. Oslo, Norway

SEIZE THE DAY

One of the best ways to make living in the real world easier later on is to use at least one year (two at max) after college to live in total fantasy. This does not mean snorting coke off hookers' backs every night (you won't be able to afford it yet), or not paying your bills, but rather allowing yourself one year to do what you have always dreamed of doing. If you have always wanted to work on a cowboy ranch, do it. If you have always wanted to teach English in a foreign country, do it. Always wanted to live in Seattle? Pack your duffel and go. Seriously. Do not worry about what will happen to you or whether this choice is directly contributing to your future. Because it definitely is, even if you can't see the connections right now.

One of the best things I did for myself was to pack a couple of suitcases and move to San Francisco a year after college graduation. I had no job there, but I found one quickly at an expensive art store, and then as a receptionist at a software  company. I had no apartment, so I stayed with my aunt in Sausalito for a month until a high school friend moved out there and we found a kick-ass place. I was in a Vespa scooter club, took a creative writing class, dated some hot Buddy Holly–looking programmers. It felt crazy and aimless at the time, but it was the best thing I ever did, A. because now I never have to say, "Gosh, I wonder what my life would be like if I lived in San Francisco," B. because now I know some awesome restaurants and places to go whenever I visit, and C. because now I know that I actually have the fortitude and wherewithal to just move across the country with nothing and make it for at least a year. This is perhaps the most important thing of all.

—*T.M.*
Atlanta, Georgia

SEE THE WORLD ON YOUR COMPANY'S DIME. I've had the good fortune of traveling to Europe about four times a year for my job, for as long as a month at a time. Not only have I gained valuable professional global experience while interfacing with my company's European offices, but I also met and fell in love with a great guy while on one of these business trips.

—*ERIN HUDAK*
AUSTIN, TEXAS

. . . .

I TOOK A LEFT TURN OUT OF COLLEGE. I was meant to go to law school and went over to England instead, working in advertising. I learned more in the first five years out of school than I did during my 80,000 college experiences. When you go through something like that, it becomes not just a book you read; you understand it. Not everyone can afford to take a year to travel overseas. But take it. It's invaluable.

—*STEFANIE*
NEW YORK, NEW YORK

. . . .

BEFORE YOU GET INVOLVED WITH SOMEONE, when you can go where *you* want to go, pick a location you have never seen and will be unlikely to see again. The only trip like this that I ever got to take was to Grand Teton National Park. I had seen a PBS special on it and couldn't get the images out of my mind. It was a spur-of-the-moment decision to go, and one I figured I'd never have the chance to do again. It was the most memorable trip I've ever taken. And I think part of that is because it was *my* trip and mine alone.

—*JAKE ELIAS*
HARRISONBURG, VIRGINIA

We live about 15 minutes from town, and let me tell you, it's no fun going back home at lunch because you forgot something!

—*BECKY*
MAGNOLIA,
ARKANSAS

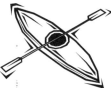

I THUMBED MY WAY ACROSS EUROPE with practically no money in my pockets. Looking back, it's a miracle that I wasn't killed. I'd take rides with anyone and sleep wherever I could. When I got desperate for money, I'd take some little job for a week and then move on. I know other people do this, but they usually have some money. I spent all I had on the flight. It was a lot of fun—the experience of a lifetime.

—CHARLENE WHITTED
JAMESTOWN, NEW YORK

• • • • • • • •

TAKE TIME TO LIVE IT UP. I traveled to random cities in the United States where I knew somebody. I didn't even have to know the person well; I just had to make sure that they extended the invitation to visit them at some point, and I took them up on the offer. My goal was to experience the nightlife in various cities around the country with new people.

—JEFF MALTZ
SAN FRANCISCO, CALIFORNIA

10 MOST EXPENSIVE U.S. CITIES

1. New York, New York
2. Boston, Massachusetts
3. Juneau, Alaska
4. Anchorage, Alaska
5. San Diego, California
6. Philadelphia, Pennsylvania
7. Los Angeles, California
8. Fairbanks, Alaska
9. Ann Arbor, Michigan
10. Seattle, Washington

SPEND THIS TIME REALIZING PERSONAL GOALS. After I was out on my own, I spent one year living away from home with no boyfriend and nothing to tie me down. After that, I was always in a relationship. I got pets. I let my world become very domestic very quickly. Because of this, I never did a lot of the traveling I wanted to do, I didn't apply to a few fellowships and writing retreats that I wanted to, I never took the time to learn Spanish—so many things that I now regret pushing aside for relationships and work.

—*B.*
CHAPEL HILL, NORTH CAROLINA

Never agree to lease a place without seeing it first.

—*ELIZABETH*
FORT WAYNE, INDIANA

DO YOUR RESEARCH. I moved to Los Angeles from Iowa shortly after I graduated, along with thousands of other recent grads. I met more than a few people my age in L.A. who were just biding time and hoping to be discovered as an actor. But if you don't do your research beforehand, set up a few job connections, and find a place to live, you're more likely to end up as the next night shift manager at Taco Bell than the next Brad Pitt.

—*JESSE AMMERMAN*
CHICAGO, ILLINOIS

WHEN YOU ARE IN YOUR NEW CITY, find all the old constellations you knew from your old city. That's very reassuring. It's something you were used to seeing before, and there it is again, right above your house. It makes the whole world seem smaller, because the people that you miss are not that far away. You're both looking at the same sky.

—*KAMI*
CAPE COD, MASSACHUSETTS

LIVE SOMEWHERE IN THE MIDDLE. Not too big, not too small. This is especially important if you are venturing out into the real world for the first time. Too big will equal a very thin wallet, a large insecurity about the friends you've acquired, and a constant yearning to fit in. Too small will equal a scarce social life, a longing to do greater things, and a head full of regrets on where you haven't been and what you haven't done.

—*KRISTI KAMERMAN*
BATON ROUGE, LOUISIANA

• • • • • • • • •

DO IT WHILE YOU'RE YOUNG

Eurailpasses are significantly cheaper for people who are under 26 years old. Check out www.raileurope.com for details.

AUSTIN, TEXAS, IS BY FAR THE BEST PLACE to live out of college. While it is not a giant city like Dallas or Houston, it offers all the draws of big-city life. However, you can drive from one side to the other in 20 minutes. It is a very eclectic town with friendly people and a unique personality. And, given that it has a huge university in the middle of it, the transition from one's college experience to the real world is easier, as the city is chock full of students and activities for young graduates.

—*ERIN HUDAK*
AUSTIN, TEXAS

• • • • • • • • •

FIND OUT WHO YOU ARE, on your own. When my dad said I could start paying him some rent money, I told him, "I would rather pay rent to someone else than to you," and went and found an apartment. It was an old building with leaded-glass windows, glass doorknobs, wood floors, and arched entryways between rooms. The place was unique and had character. It was nice to have a neat place where friends could come hang out and party without bugging my parents.

—*BRETT*
CHICAGO, ILLINOIS

EASY AS 1, 2, 3

Most people totally freak out after graduating from college; many to the point where they end up moving back in with their parents. I don't get it. It's really not that bad.

Step One: Decide what you want—to be close to family or friends, to meet new people, to have nice weather or specific job opportunities.

Step Two: Move to the place where you can get that. Get a job. It doesn't matter what kind. Anyone can find enough work to pay the bills, especially if you have a college education. If the job sucks, work until you find something better.

Step Three: Work your way up until you have the career you want, or enough money to go back to school or to travel or whatever.

It's really that simple. Set some goals; *do* things. It's better than hanging out in your mom's basement.

—*Fred*
Washington, D.C.

READY TO SEE THE WORLD?

Check out the State Department site for passport and visa requirements for each country: travel.state.gov.

THE BEST ADVICE MY DAD ever gave me was "Once you graduate from college, move to the place you want to live and then find a job. Don't let your job dictate where you live, if you can afford it." I wanted to live in California, so I moved there out of college. My first apartment was a 400-square-foot studio that only had room for a minifridge, not even a real freezer. I lived there for four years, but eventually I moved into a two-bedroom apartment. And now, I actually own my own condo in Southern California, so I'm finally "in." I never could have done it if I took a job in Chicago (where I went to college) and then tried to move to San Diego. It's the best advice my dad could have given me, and I love every minute of it!

—*ANONYMOUS*
SAN DIEGO, CALIFORNIA

• • • • • • • •

NEW YORK CITY! Coming from the West Coast—Seattle and the Bay Area—New York is a whirlwind where you can learn and be anonymous if you need to. Check out craigslist.org or other boards, and try to line up a job before moving out. Then try to crash for a few weeks with your brother's friend's cousin, or someone like that, while you find a place to live. Search for digs downtown and don't rule out Brooklyn. You might get a better deal on a place and still have incredible access to the energy of the Big Apple.

—*JENNIFER*
SEATTLE, WASHINGTON

THE TWO MOST IMPORTANT FACTORS in choosing a place to live out of college are price and location relative to activity. It is tempting to look at that five-figure salary on your offer letter and then go shopping for the apartment you always wanted but couldn't afford. Don't make a move until you put pen to paper. Research the cost of utilities, phone, cell phone, Internet access, cable, renter's insurance, car payment, vehicle insurance, and so on. Create a budget and decide what is reasonable for monthly rent. After that, try to find a place in your budget where you'll find activities for young people. Usually, it's closer to the center of the metropolitan area rather than way out in the suburbs, where families mostly live.

—JAMES RINEY
FORT WORTH, TEXAS

. . . .

MY FIRST POSTCOLLEGE HOUSE was a little rental on the south side—the poor side—of Ottumwa, Iowa. I paid $300 a month for this place, and that was actually a huge chunk of my monthly income. My first job as a copy editor for the local newspaper didn't pay all that much. I remember telling myself that to be able to enjoy the other parts of my life, I'd have to live in a cheaper part of town. That ended up being a great decision. My little blue one-bedroom house eventually became somewhat of a party place. I made it my own and people loved to come over for barbecues, ice-cold beer, and my famous Bloody Marys. Even though I didn't have much, I made the best of it, and I learned many valuable lessons just by sacrificing a little bit of comfort and style to live within my means.

—E.E.
ST. LOUIS, MISSOURI

Americans think it's a big deal to move to a foreign country, but people who live outside of the United States think nothing of it.

—BILLIE
CHICAGO, ILLINOIS

APARTMENT HUNTING 101

You can't take road trips forever. Sooner or later, you'll have to settle down in one place, and for the recently graduated, that usually means finding an apartment. Here are some proven tips to help you along.

BEFORE YOU SIGN A LEASE ON AN APARTMENT, find out how flexible the landlord will be on the length of the lease. Most leases are for one year, but the attitudes of landlords vary. If you are planning to buy a home in six months and your rental lease is for one year, you will likely lose your security deposit if you break the lease. My landlord agreed on a month-to-month lease agreement after the first six months. I think he was agreeable to it because I was up front with him about my plans and didn't just sneak out in the middle of the night.

—*ANONYMOUS*
STRONGSVILLE, OHIO

WHEN YOU ARE PICKING A PLACE TO LIVE, it is important to make sure it has sufficient storage space. The longer you are out of college, the more stuff you accumulate. If you know you are not disciplined about getting rid of stuff, just prepare for it.

—*JOSH*
WEST PLAINS, MISSOURI

I STARTED OFF BY RENTING A CHEAP APARTMENT, which was the best decision I could have made. I had no real concept of bills—how much they would cost or the costs of living on my own in general. I think if I had settled on a nicer apartment I wouldn't have been able to afford it.

—*I.B.*
INDIANAPOLIS, INDIANA

ON APARTMENTRATINGS.COM, current and former tenants of complexes nationwide share their experiences living in particular places. The site is pretty accurate, too. When I logged on to check out a complex I'd just moved out of, I saw their satisfaction rating was only 25 percent. This was completely fitting, considering that, after I broke my lease, they chose to withhold my security deposit (even though there was no damage) and about $2,500 extra.

—*R.W.*
FORT COLLINS, COLORADO

• • • • • • • • •

JUST BECAUSE A LANDLORD ASKS FOR A DEPOSIT or the lease says a deposit is required, don't feel that this item is nonnegotiable. Everything, including the rent, is negotiable. It depends on how badly they need to rent the space out. Look for apartment complexes that have lots of vacancies. Those landlords will be more willing to work with you on some of those issues just to get you in there.

—*BRETT DAVID*
HARRISONBURG, VIRGINIA

IT PAYS OFF TO PUSH OUTSIDE the comfort zone of home. After I finished my master's degree in communications, I was desperate to start my life. I didn't want to fall into the proverbial black hole in my hometown, where college grads came home to live at their parents' houses and work at Starbucks because they were too afraid to leave their safety zones. It is really hard at first, but sticking it out is worth it.

—*CHERYL*
PHILADELPHIA, PENNSYLVANIA

. . . .

"Register for automatic e-mail updates on super-saver fares from airlines. I get weekly e-mails from Delta, American, United—you name it. I once saved $200 on a flight that way."

—*STEVE GEHN*
GERRY, NEW YORK

. . . .

DON'T BE AFRAID TO MOVE OUT OF STATE for a job. My hometown had 6,000 people in it; I wanted something larger. I had a job offer from a place where I had interned, in Wisconsin, but I didn't want to stay there forever. I like big cities. So I turned it down and cast a wider net.

—*MARCELLE HENDRICKS*
WESTMINSTER, COLORADO

NEVER MOVE OUT ON YOUR OWN unless you have saved up *at least* $3,000. I moved from New York to Georgia after college. I thought it would be easy considering how much you get for your dollar in Georgia compared to New York. But even the low rent was something I could not afford. I also found out the hard way that public transportation in Georgia is darn near nonexistent. I am a city girl, and I found myself walking country dirt roads trying to get to work. So, two things: 1. Make sure you research a new town before your big move, and 2. *Stay away from Georgia!* Just kidding. But adequately prepare your finances, or you will find yourself in a bind and it'll be back to Mom and Dad's for you!

—*Q.S.*
NEW YORK, NEW YORK

• • • • • • • •

WHEN I GRADUATED FROM ART SCHOOL, it seemed like the natural thing to do was to move to New York. I resisted this idea for a long time prior to graduating, but then I realized that if I wanted the exposure to other people who were actually making art to support themselves, this was the place to be. I absolutely love it here. In the nearly five years I have lived here, I have had to shed a lot of the romantic ideas about starving artists eating raw noodles just long enough to make that one great painting that puts them on the map. It can be done that way, but more than likely you will want to live in a place that is semi-rodent-free and go out for the occasional cocktail with the thousands of other artists trying to make it in this city.

—*CHARLES*
BROOKLYN, NEW YORK

DON'T FOLLOW SOMEONE BECAUSE you're in love with them. When I graduated college, I followed my boyfriend to this town because he wanted to be a musician, and he thought it was the right place for him to be. Of course there was nothing there for me, and I ended up waiting tables for 10 years in that town. No man is worth that.

—J.
BINGHAMTON, NEW YORK

" Do you actually think your future boss or spouse is going to let you take three months off to hit Eurail? Go now, while you're free from obligations. "

—J.A.
ATLANTA, GEORGIA

IF YOU CAN FIGURE OUT A WAY TO GO ABROAD, do it. You will experience things that will never happen to you in the States. I went to Spain with some friends and we wanted to go to Pamplona to see the running of the bulls. We needed a ride there. We were about two hours away, and we caught a ride with this guy with an 18-wheeler. I wouldn't be caught dead riding in an 18-wheeler in the United States. You'd be chopped up into little pieces. But for some reason, it was OK in Spain.

—LEANNE
ATLANTA, GEORGIA

IF YOU WENT TO SCHOOL in a college town, move away once you graduate. College towns have this strange thing about them where people who stay there after school think it's OK to act like they are still in school but without the learning part. I know so many bright people who graduated and then just hung around, drinking and playing in bands and working in restaurants. The same thing could have happened to me, but I moved to New York and went to grad school. Being in a city like that made me really understand the value of ambition.

> —*LIZ*
> *GREENVILLE, NORTH CAROLINA*

A GOOD WAY TO FIND AN APARTMENT is to just drive to areas you'd like to live and look for "For Rent" signs there. I did it, and it helped me learn my way around. This is better than reading the classified ads and then wasting your time going to a place only to find out it's somewhere you'd never want to live.

> —*J.R.*
> *FREDERICK, MARYLAND*

IF YOU'VE NEVER BEEN TO EUROPE, you can get yourself a Eurail pass and see some of the world's most famous places. Do it before you're 26, because that's the age when you can longer get "youth" discounts. I saw places that everybody talks about, like Paris and Rome. It makes me feel more like a part of the adult world.

> —*CLARE*
> *SEATTLE, WASHINGTON*

DO SOMETHING CRAZY. Once, my friends and I bought these supercheap airline tickets from Southwest. We flew down to San Diego and then rented a car and drove down to Mexico. We only bought the plane tickets one way, and then we didn't have enough money to fly back, so we had to take the rental car and drive it from Mexico the whole way to Kentucky. We almost didn't even have enough money to do that. When we got back, I think we had about $17 left between us. But it was a superfun trip. When you are 21 years old, I can't think of a better place to go.

—CARLOS ZAHIR
INDEPENDENCE, KENTUCKY

• • • • • • • •

YOU COULD GO TO A MILLION PLACES that cost a ton of money. Or you could do something that's perfect for a college grad—cheap, adventurous, and best done before you have major responsibilities. I'm talking about the great U.S. national parks. I went camping and hiking for a whole summer with my best college buddies through Bryce, Arches, Zion, and the Grand Canyon, and it is still one of the greatest memories.

—SAM
SANTA MONICA, CALIFORNIA

• • • • • • • •

CAP YOUR COLLEGE EXPERIENCE with a summer trip with your best friends. It's pretty painful to graduate and leave "the best years of your life," so I recommend something fun to ease the transition. My roommates and I hit a beach on Jamaica, drank frou-frou cocktails, and flirted with guys for a week. It was awesome.

—DENISE
BOSTON, MASSACHUSETTS

AFTER COLLEGE, I BACKPACKED around Asia for almost a year. Even though I started out alone, I met up with great people and had travel partners when I wanted them. I did beaches, temples, great natural sites, and partied like a rock star, all in places that are way off the map and cheap, cheap, cheap. My favorite countries were Vietnam and Indonesia, but everybody loves someplace different. Take a trip like this while you've got the time and energy.

—*J.R.*
CHICAGO, ILLINOIS

• • • • • • • •

USE YOUR ALUMNI NETWORKS (online groups and local alumni associations) to find recent grads with rooms for rent. You're more likely to find someone who's got something in common with you, and if you're moving to a far-off city, it's nice to have a roommate who knows what you're going through.

—*JERRY*
NEW YORK, NEW YORK

• • • • • • • •

DON'T LIVE WITH OLD GRADE SCHOOL and high school friends unless you've been closely in touch with them all through college. I moved back to my hometown and thought it'd be great to room with my old friends. Well, we'd all changed a ton and had nothing in common anymore. It was pretty uncomfortable, and I wished I'd just roomed with strangers instead.

—*CARL*
MINNEAPOLIS, MINNESOTA

WHEN LOOKING AT AN APARTMENT, don't get suckered in by fresh paint or carpet. Make sure you bring along somebody who knows about housing. I ended up in a freshly painted and carpeted rathole with major cockroaches, stopped-up toilets, and mildew everywhere. At the time, I was so proud of myself for finding it. Then the first time my Dad walked through, he pointed out all of those things that did, in fact, become huge problems for me.

—C.C.
RENO, NEVADA

• • • • • • • • •

DON'T ASSUME that the monthly rent figure that you are quoted is set in stone. Feel free to try to negotiate it with the landlord. Why not? What have you got to lose? Ask them if they would take less; if they won't, ask them if you could get a discount for paying early each month. You never know if you don't ask.

—*TRINA AMAKER*
NIKEP, MARYLAND

Dealing With Others: Your Parents, Your Roommates

By some estimates, 60 percent of college graduates return home after graduation. Whether they can stand to stay longer than a month is a different issue. As you'll read in this chapter, dealing with your parents after college can be a challenge. If you're living with them, you'll inevitably have rules to follow. If you live away from them, you'll need to keep in touch and set boundaries. And speaking of boundaries: Enter the roommate. Assuming yours is not psycho, there are still some trials that await you as you try to carve out a new life for yourself while sharing cramped space with someone else.

PEOPLE ARE LIKE DOGS; they need to be trained. Your parents think you are irresponsible. Could it be your $100 tab at the bar and you subsequently asking them for money to cover rent? Listen to your parents so they can train you.

—J.
WASHINGTON, D.C.

LIVE AT HOME, WHERE EVERYTHING IS FREE.

—B.M.
ZIRKLE, VIRGINIA

HEADLINES
Best Advice and Top Tips

- Live at home as long as you can—it's free!
- Roommates can help you meet new people.
- Embrace your independence—don't move back in with your parents.
- Living alone means a lot less hassle in your life.
- If you move away from home, make an effort to stay in close contact with your parents.

Roommates are good for stealing food and then playing dumb: "What cake?"

—MATTHEW WISE
TORONTO,
ONTARIO, CANADA

IT'S HARD FOR EVERYONE when you go back home because your parents still see you as their child, and you want to be independent. If you can avoid moving home, it is best to get your own place. After I graduated from college, I moved back home to St. Louis and stayed with my parents. I love my parents, but it was an awful experience for all of us. I wanted total freedom, to go out with my friends and come home when I pleased. My dad, however, felt that I should not stay out late. He told me that if I wanted to live under his roof, I had to follow his rules. I moved out after six months. We were all happier once I did.

—JACKIE MOORE
OZARK, MISSOURI

BE INDEPENDENT. Don't move back with your parents. I did. It was a nightmare. You are used to all this freedom, but then you're back under their roof with their rules. It was a major power struggle. I moved out and moved in with a boyfriend. Bad move. I got married and got divorced. Stand on your own two feet when you get out of college. It's easier to struggle earlier in life than later on.

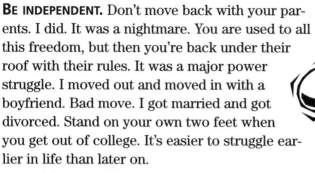

—*ANONYMOUS*
NEW YORK, NEW YORK

66 Don't expect your roommate to be a family subsitute. He or she may have a very different idea of what a household is...of what a home is. 99

—*N.*
BROOKLYN, NEW YORK

LIVE AT HOME. I didn't have a high-paying first job, so I needed to live at home with my parents for a year. But I think it helped make the transition from college to the "real world" a little easier. Plus, my mom is a good cook and I hate doing laundry.

—*JIM*
HOBOKEN, NEW JERSEY

TRY TO REMEMBER THE THINGS your parents taught you. When I was first living out on my own and I faced a moral question, I would always stop and wonder what my parents would think about my decision. Would they approve? Those answers aren't always going to make you happy, but more often than not they will be the right things to do.

—*JONATHAN GRESH*
POLAND, OHIO

· · · · · · · ·

Use your parents as a sounding board as you go through large and important decisions. You don't have to listen to their advice, but it helps to be able to talk these things out with someone who's been there.

—*T.W.*
YOUNGSTOWN, OHIO

· · · · · · · ·

LIVE WITH YOUR PARENTS until you can live on your own. I lived with my parents for a couple of years because in my industry, television, you don't necessarily get a full-time job right away. It took me a few years to get comfortable and get a steady enough gig and income to justify getting my own place.

—*JOSH TIZEL*
TORONTO, ONTARIO, CANADA

APPRECIATE HOW YOUR RELATIONSHIP changes with your parents. When I was in college, I was much more dependent on my parents to help me make the right choices and decisions. They were the ones giving me advice on life issues. After college, things began to change. I moved out to start a life of my own. As I became more experienced in life, I became more independent. I also found that when I spent time with my parents, I was formulating friendships with them. I have experienced some things they haven't and have been able to give them advice on certain things. I love to share with my parents as well as learn from them.

—*CHERI*
MUNCIE, INDIANA

· · · · · · · ·

BE PREPARED FOR YOUR RELATIONSHIP with your parents to do a complete 180. My parents and I were never friends when I was in my teens. We battled out every issue in a full-on war. But as I progressed into my 20s and became more independent and more able to financially support myself, our relationship changed. We are now good friends. I call my mom every week just to hear how things are going.

—*HEATHER POLLOCK*
ORANGE COUNTY, CALIFORNIA

Living with your parents? Family effort is essential to survival in places like Japan; they are among the most efficient of civilizations.

—*LOUIS HAGMAN*
SEATTLE,
WASHINGTON

FIND THE MIDDLE GROUND. I totally shut my parents out after college. They didn't agree with the choices I was making, and so I did the whole "I'm an adult now, and you can't tell me what to do" bit. It's amazing, isn't it, how we can feel totally justified telling them to leave us alone? I think there can be a middle ground, where you take responsibility for yourself without shutting out the people who care about you.

—*J.*
BINGHAMTON, NEW YORK

• • • • • • • • •

KEEP IN TOUCH WITH YOUR PARENTS. My mom has always been my best friend, and when I moved out three years ago I had horrible separation anxiety. Talking on the phone once a day with her helps tremendously.

—*AFFTON BOEHLE*
ST. LOUIS, MISSOURI

ESSENTIALS FOR YOUR FIRST APARTMENT

1. Mattress/bed
2. Trash cans
3. Shower curtain and shower rings
4. Curtains or blinds
5. Chest of drawers or hanging closet organizers
6. Dishware, cups and utensils
7. Table and/or desk
8. Chair
9. Lamp
10. Bookshelf
11. Sofa or futon

THE BEST THING YOU can ask prospective room-mates is what television shows they like to watch. You can learn a lot about people this way. Someone who loves nothing but horror movies and slasher films might be someone to avoid. You don't want to be involved in a yearlong lease with someone who turns out to be an escaped mental patient.

> —*BENNY TADFORD*
> *YOUNGSTOWN, OHIO*

• • • • • • • •

IT IS GOOD TO KEEP IN CONTACT with your parents because they enjoy it, and usually there is a good meal waiting for you at home. Give a call to say you're OK. Or if you're in their area, drop in from time to time to catch up and eat well.

> —*LOUIS HAGMAN*
> *SEATTLE, WASHINGTON*

• • • • • • • •

YOU MUST CONSIDER your roommate's needs and expectations. You can't simply enter a roommate situation and think, "I'll stay the same and hope it works." There's going to be compromise and you have to know that going in.

> —*MUCI*
> *TORONTO, ONTARIO, CANADA*

• • • • • • • •

WHEN LIVING WITH SOMEONE, make sure they know that the Snickers bar in the fridge is yours. Once, I was at work all day, thinking about eating that Snickers bar in the fridge when I got home. But when I got there, you guessed it—my room-mate had eaten it. She even thanked me!

> —*MICHELE*
> *HOLLY, MICHIGAN*

Don't live with a friend, but find an apart-ment in the same building as a friend. That way, you're not alone, but you have your space.

> —*SHARON HAROWITZ*
> *VANCOUVER, BRITISH COLUMBIA, CANADA*

LIVE ON YOUR OWN AFTER GETTING A JOB. I wanted independence and living with a roommate felt too much like college. I didn't want to have to depend on anyone else or worry about someone else not paying their share. It was hard, but it was worth it.

—*WENDY*
ALLENTOWN, PENNSYLVANIA

. . . .

" Living alone is the way to go. I have a three-bedroom place for just my dog and me. There is so much less hassle. If there's a mess to clean up, it's my mess. If the music is too loud, I can turn it down. "

—*T.J.K.*
WESTMINSTER, CALIFORNIA

. . . .

DON'T LIVE WITH A GOOD FRIEND and don't live with a complete stranger. It's best to live with someone you're connected to and that you know but that you're not that close with. If you live with a good friend, you run the risk of losing the closeness of the friendship and starting to see the person as a roommate who occasionally does annoying things.

—*VERONICA*
TORONTO, ONTARIO, CANADA

ROOMMATES HELP YOU GROW. I didn't have roommates for three years in Japan, so I lived in isolation, slowly going mad with my quirks and tendencies. It wasn't until I moved to Toronto and had roommates that I experienced that mirror: a chance to have all my weird traits reflected back at me. Suddenly, my quirks became apparent, and it forced me to reevaluate how obsessive I had become in my own little environment.

—*DARCY BELANGER*
SHERWOOD PARK, ALBERTA, CANADA

TAKE THE HELP YOUR PARENTS OFFER YOU. I saw so many of my friends try to be tough and tell their parents to bugger off when they were really still kids who didn't know how to handle the world yet. I did the opposite. I went home to live with my parents twice after I moved out. I asked for advice; I asked for money. And now I am closer to my parents than most people I know. It's good for me and for them. We are still a family.

—*SARAH*
WEST HARTFORD, CONNECTICUT

AFTER YOU MOVE OUT, make sure you call home at least once a week. Don't do it for your dad; he probably won't even realize you're gone. But do it for your mother. Believe me, she'll be missing you and thinking about you all the time. I used to call my mom late every Sunday night. I could hear the sparkle in her voice across the phone lines. Take the time to pick up the phone and make her day.

—*HENRY ANDERSON*
BOARDMAN, OHIO

HOME IS WHERE THE GRADUATE IS

In a survey done by monster.com a few years ago, more than 60 percent of college seniors planned to return home after graduation.

WHEN LOOKING FOR A ROOMMATE: If someone else has had trouble living with a person you're considering for a roommate, there is usually a reason why.

—*ELIZABETH*
PHILADELPHIA, PENNSYLVANIA

. . . .

HOW TO COMMUNICATE WITH YOUR PARENTS: Therapy seemed to work. I figured out how to talk to them.

—*ANONYMOUS*
SITKA, ALASKA

. . . .

WHEN YOUR PARENTS SAY, "Make yourself at home," use your best judgment. They don't want you to hang around and mooch for months.

—*CHERI RIOT*
MISSION VIEJO, CALIFORNIA

. . . .

THE BENEFITS OF LIVING with your parents: free food, free laundry, no rent. The drawbacks: coming up with explanations after you go out on a Friday night and stumble back in the next afternoon reeking of booze and cheap perfume.

—*JESSE AMMERMAN*
IOWA CITY, IOWA

When your parents say, "Make yourself at home," use your best judgment. They don't want you to hang around and mooch for months.

—*CHERI RIOT*
MISSION VIEJO,
CALIFORNIA

You're Hired: Finding Your First Real Job

So you want to be Donald Trump? Or Martha Stewart (sans the jail sentence)? Or maybe even Diane Fosse or Bono? Good for you; dream big and set goals. Now, about that first job. It's the first step in what will undoubtedly be a highly successful career. Perhaps you know what line of work you want to be in; perhaps you are like millions of others who are still figuring it out. But this rite of passage into the real world—interviewing for a job, getting a job—is at hand. While there are countless books offering expert advice on résumés and interview techniques, we offer tales from the trenches.

HOW DID I FIGURE OUT what to do with my life? I've been out of school for five years and I'm still figuring it out!

—*MARIANA*
SAN FRANCISCO, CALIFORNIA

THERE'S SOMETHING OUT THERE; IT'S JUST A MATTER OF BEING RESOURCEFUL.

—*LISA OLKON*
VANDESTEEG
ST. PAUL, MINNESOTA

HEAD LINES
Best Advice and Top Tips

- Do your research—find out as much as you can about the field you're interested in.

- Network, network, network—contact people in the industry to make important connections.

- Don't expect to start at the top—entry-level jobs allow you to really learn the business.

- The job interview is also your chance to check out the company—make sure it feels like the right environment.

- As soon as you get home from your interview, sit down and write a thank-you.

FIGURE OUT WHAT YOU DESIRE OUT OF LIFE. Take the time to figure out what motivates you and what makes you happy. That can take some trial and error. The people that I know who love their careers are the people who struggled a bit to get there. I didn't know where I wanted to go with my life until after college. I had been an anthropology major, and I was interested in documentary work, but I was still searching for the right path. After some traveling and soul searching for a few months, I solidified my desire to become a photographer. It took time and patience and working lots of part-time jobs while I took classes and developed my skills.

—*L.G.*
DURHAM, NORTH CAROLINA

WHEN SEARCHING FOR A JOB, plan ahead more than I did. I knew I wanted to get into advertising, but I didn't know anyone in the industry and had no idea how to find a job in advertising. I wound up replying to an ad in the Sunday paper and landing a job at J. Walter Thompson as an administrative assistant. I lucked out: JWT is a great ad agency, and I wound up working there for almost five years.

> —ANONYMOUS
> NEW YORK, NEW YORK

• • • • • • • •

"Prepare for a job interview like you're making a 30-second commercial of yourself. Make sure your story is clear, to the point, and flows smoothly from beginning to end. Most important, rehearse!"

> —JEFF CELLIO
> LAGUNA NIGUEL, CALIFORNIA

• • • • • • • •

YOU ARE A FUNGIBLE WORKER BEE. Get over your pride and use your connections. "Referred by so-and-so's tennis partner" scrawled by the HR person at the top of your résumé may be the only thing separating you from the other fungible worker bees.

> —D.M.
> NEW YORK, NEW YORK

MEET AS MANY PEOPLE AS YOU can who work in the industry you want to break into. I wrote a number of e-mails to contacts and asked if I could take them out for a quick coffee and discussion. I always mentioned the fact that I would love their good insight, and I think most were flattered. It's true that "important" people are busy, but many people like to feel like they have influence and are admired; many will take time out of their day to share their story with you. It's more important in these meetings to ask questions than to sell yourself. Remember, it's not a job interview; it's a chance to show how committed you are to pursuing your goals and learning about the industry. You'd be surprised: Many of these meetings lead to a job later on, or a good referral to another person in the field who may have work for you.

—*ANDREA*
TORONTO, ONTARIO, CANADA

THE ODDS ARE GETTING BETTER

Employers expect to hire 14.5 percent more new college graduates in 2006 than they hired in 2005.

DO RESEARCH ON DIFFERENT JOBS. Find out how much jobs pay, what skills are required, and what a typical day would look like. A job might seem attractive, but when you learn the day-to-day workings of it, you might change your mind.

—*CHRISTOPHER*
HAVERTOWN, PENNSYLVANIA

THE DAMN GOOD RÉSUMÉ GUIDE is the only book anybody should ever use to help them write a resume. It took me through both the chronological and functional formats and taught me how to do a skills inventory and write out my exact qualifications in a marketable fashion. I've actually had several people compliment my resume.

—*R.W.*
FORT COLLINS, COLORADO

DON'T EXPECT THAT DREAM JOB RIGHT AWAY. If you are willing to do the grunt-work jobs, you will learn the business. And if you give it your all, most likely you will be rewarded for your efforts. My bachelor's degree was in art history, so I literally knocked on gallery doors in Cincinnati, where I was living, armed with my résumé and a don't-take-no-for-an-answer attitude. I started out helping out around a gallery and driving the owner's daughters to and from swim practice. I was running the entire business by the end of the summer.

—*DEIRDRE MORGANTHALER*
CASTLE ROCK, COLORADO

• • • • • • • •

DON'T SCRIMP ON THE QUALITY OF PAPER you use for your résumé. Trust me, I have an aunt who works in HR; it matters. I know it seems crazy to spend that kind of money for a thicker, better-looking piece of paper. But if you ultimately get the job, it's worth it. And buy cream-colored. Never white. It will make it stand out from the others.

—*ANONYMOUS*
SOUTH BEND, INDIANA

✔

Arrive at the interview with a box of doughnuts for the office.

—*SHARON HAROWITZ*
VANCOUVER, BRITISH COLUMBIA, CANADA

AVOIDING THE DAILY GRIND

Not ready to commit to a 9-to-5 career? Here are a few productive distractions:

Peace Corps, www.peacecorps.gov.
Freelance work, www.freelanceworkexchange.com
Work abroad,www.transitionsabroad.com/listings/work/index.shtml
AmeriCorps, www.americorps.org

A LEAP FROM LIBERAL ARTS TO LAW

Don't limit yourself with a preset career path. I never thought I would be considered for a high-paying corporate law job. I was an art history major at a liberal arts college, and I didn't know the first thing about finance or corporate law. I did manage to get into law school, though, and my parents were telling me to think about representing children.

After I got to law school, I found out that if you get a certain GPA your first year, the law firms track you down and throw jobs at you. Who knew? So I took a summer position because the money was good, and then I found out finance is actually pretty interesting, especially when combined with all the recent corporate scandals. Who knew again?

So I took a permanent offer after graduation. The law firm probably won't be my final destination because the hours are hellacious, but I am confident that working there will present some other opportunity I hadn't thought of before, just like law school did. It's like going from one handle to the next on the monkey bars.

　　—D.M.
　　NEW YORK, NEW YORK

FIND WHAT INTERESTS YOU and be willing to work for free in an internship or something. I was a photojournalist and went to a paper out of college and told them I'd work for free. It took a few months for them to realize they should hire me, but I ended up getting a great job shooting for United Press International.

—PAUL DIAMOND
SEATTLE, WASHINGTON

> Be upbeat, positive, and cheerful at your interview. Don't let any negativity slide into your voice or your body language. Paint a freakin' clown smile on your face for that hour and keep it there. It's contagious.

—LORNA MERKEIL
ELLSWORTH, OHIO

ALWAYS BE ON YOUR BEST BEHAVIOR when you are on a job interview. But also consider it your opportunity to interview the company. I had four job offers. I went with the one with the best salary. It was a good experience, but it wasn't the right fit for me. I've since learned that it is important to hold out for a work environment that you enjoy. It may not be the one that offers the best paycheck. In the long run, it will be worth it.

—BILLIE
CHICAGO, ILLINOIS

Do what you enjoy or you won't *have* a life after college.

—J. KYLE KISER
SCOTTSDALE,
ARIZONA

USE YOUR PROFESSORS AS RESOURCES. After college, I went to Europe for four months, and when I came back, I scheduled a meeting with my favorite professor. I asked him if he had any suggestions on how I should move forward after graduation. This professor helped me. He knew somebody at a PR firm and called his contact for me. This led to my first job after college!

—*MARIANA*
SAN FRANCISCO, CALIFORNIA

❝Remain calm. If you're nervous, get that emotion under control. I always use the technique Mr. Brady taught Marcia on *The Brady Bunch:* Picture the interviewer in his underwear.❞

—*J.B.*
DEERFIELD, OHIO

IF AN IT RECRUITER GIVES YOU a technical assessment that asks you specific IT-related questions, don't tell him that you haven't read a technical book in a long time. To be successful in IT, you must constantly read about new technologies. Do your homework. Research the company and brush up on some of your skills.

—*Z.E.*
NEW SPRINGFIELD, OHIO

I WANT A RAISE! BEFORE I START!

For your first professional job out of college, I don't think negotiating salary is much of an option. You really have no power in this negotiation. You need to get busy building your resume more than they need you. I made the mistake of asking for a few thousand dollars more with a job, and then I didn't get it. A friend of mine later told me to keep in mind that the person making the offer is not the person who set the salary or who has the power to give you more money. This is especially true in big companies. By asking for more  money, you are putting that person in a bad position because they have to go back to their boss with your counterproposal. It's not a good situation. Later in your career you will be able to wheel and deal. But not with the first job.

—TRAVIS LINDEN
HARRISONBURG, VIRGINIA

USING INTERNSHIPS

After I graduated, many fields of work were tight and had few jobs available, so I used the time to work in internships. The internships were helpful because I was able to be employed while looking for a permanent position or another internship. I did four or five internships (each about four to six months long). I sought out internships at places well-known in my field, photojournalism, and places that had the reputation for hosting the best internship programs.

Also, network with friends in the field. Find out where your friends or people you meet have interned, and apply to that internship. I know that a lot of students I worked with at the paper in college were interning each year with companies that previously hired students from our school. Many employers are impressed by students who previously worked for them, and they will go back to that school to find more employees.

    —*BRETT*
    CHICAGO, ILLINOIS

CLASSIFIED ADS SUCK. Most quality jobs aren't advertised in newspapers. I've found 80 percent of my positions via networking and going through recruiters who found my résumé on monster.com.

—ROBERT SALTER
MÖNCHENGLADBACH, GERMANY

IT'S ABOUT WHO YOU KNOW. Most of the really good jobs aren't even advertised. I got hired at my current job because one of my friends was the manager. That's the way the world works.

—D.S.
DENVER, COLORADO

"Always wear a suit to an interview, even if the job won't require you to wear one. The difference in your appearance is amazing. Wearing a suit gives me more confidence."

—ANONYMOUS
SAN DIEGO, CALIFORNIA

GET YOUR FOOT IN THE DOOR. I had interned at the same place where I ended up getting my first job. The company was being uprooted to a new location, and they were really hurting for people. They brought me in as a temp.

—ANONYMOUS
BROOKLYN, NEW YORK

NETWORKING ISN'T JUST A FORMAL THING, it can also take place through social outlets. I belong to a church. I didn't have a job, and one day, these people from my church called and asked me to do Web editing for their vacation rental Web site. I set my own schedule, which is very cool. I absolutely love it.

—*AFFTON BOEHLE*
ST. LOUIS, MISSOURI

· · · · · · · ·

YOU ARE NOT ALONE

In 2005, an estimated 1.4 million college graduates entered the workforce.

DON'T GO INTO A JOB INTERVIEW knowing more than your potential boss. I once did a lot of research before an interview, and I clearly made a potential employer uncomfortable when I brought things up that he wasn't prepared to discuss. Keep in mind that while you want to impress the staff at the office, many people are insecure about losing their jobs and may be scared of competition. So, in a job interview, show that you're willing to learn. Show ambition but don't ever say something like, "I want to learn to run my own business one day."

—*MATTHEW WISE*
TORONTO, ONTARIO, CANADA

· · · · · · · ·

USE ALUMNI ASSOCIATIONS. My college found my first job for me. The school had an outplacement program that didn't cost me a dime. All I had to do was meet with a counselor to tell what sort of work I was looking for, what field my degree was in, and what kind of money I was looking for. That was it. They would periodically mail job openings to me that they felt were a good fit. Those people are usually well connected with the business community in their area, so this can be a big help.

—*MATT TIMMONS*
CALLA, OHIO

GET IN ON THE GROUND FLOOR. I was going to graduate school for education, and I knew I wanted to find something related to kids. I found an ad for a company, and I originally went to work as a tutor for them. Then things happened! I became a teacher at the new school they were starting, working 25 hours a week in the beginning. Eventually I moved into the administrative offices. Three years later I was the dean of students at the school, which had grown from a handful of students to something like 85.

—REBECCA SHENN
NEW YORK, NEW YORK

• • • • • • • •

" Find a career that has the potential of earning you money, but do something you're interested in. At the end of the day, what people strive for is happiness. "

—JANNA
TORONTO, ONTARIO, CANADA

• • • • • • • •

FIND FRIENDS WHO LIKE THEIR JOBS. I got the best job I ever had through a friend, and it's a job I never would have gotten otherwise. People think of networking as trying to chat up people you don't know, but it's as simple as contacting the people you already know and letting them know you need a job.

—CHRISTINA
CHAPEL HILL, NORTH CAROLINA

HOW I STARTED IN PUBLIC RADIO

When I moved to Atlanta right out of Cornell, I had a Dodge Colt, a beautiful but flaky girlfriend, and a business degree. While having to sell off my record collection piece by piece in order to afford groceries, my girlfriend soon left me for a CPA earning $150K a year. That left me with only a car—which burst into flames on a Sunday-morning drive to Krispy Kreme.

I was able to get another car with a cosign from my mother. I immediately took it on a long road trip, sleeping in the car and on friends' couches. Driving home from New York, I heard a short story being read on the radio and decided to launch a literary magazine in audio format. Some friends and I put together a couple hundred bucks and launched it out of my apartment.

When the first issue came out, we were covered by NPR's *Morning Edition* and had a full-page story in *Publisher's Weekly*. Because of that coverage, an author contacted me and asked me to create a public radio program out of his book of inter-  views. Two weeks later, I was in the Hamptons at a party with the New York scene, including Kurt Vonnegut, Jay McInerney, and Sidney Lumet. Oscar winner Cliff Robertson agreed to host the program, AT&T agreed to sponsor, and NPR picked up the show.

I tried a "real" job after that, but I was miserable. I soon found someone else to sponsor a radio series, and I have been making a good living producing radio since.

The moral is to do something, anything. If you start moving forward, doors will open. More than anything, creativity is what drives the American economy. If you demonstrate practical creative thinking, people will track you down.

—*Daren*
Decatur, Georgia

KNOW PEOPLE IN THE RIGHT PLACES or get your foot in the door somehow. This is a better way to introduce yourself to a company than by storming the HR office with a baseball bat.

—*JESSE AMMERMAN*
IOWA CITY, IOWA

NETWORKING IS A TERM YOU NEED to become familiar with. And, no, it doesn't mean clicking from NBC to CBS to ABC.

—*BOB MAGYARICS*
CALLA, OHIO

IN ANY INTERVIEW, when they ask what your "worst" qualities are, tell them something that can be good, like, "Sometimes I'm a little too detailed."

—*LISA OLKON VANDESTEEG*
ST PAUL, MINNESOTA

ALL OF MY REALLY GREAT TEACHING JOBS have come from education fairs. I've found that when you meet the recruiter in person and have that personal contact, it makes a huge difference.

—*ELIZABETH*
FORT WAYNE, INDIANA

66 Spell-check your cover letters. I received one cover letter back and the woman had taken a red pen to it. I was like, "Oh, let me eat my piece of humble pie." Apparently seven years of college hasn't taught me much. 99

—*LEANNE*
ATLANTA, GEORGIA

YOU SHOULD NEVER DISQUALIFY any experience you have. You never know where something is going to lead. I went to school for religion and philosophy, but I put myself through school by cooking. After I graduated, I kept cooking because I enjoyed it and because it's what I was most qualified to do. Now, I have a pretty good career as a chef.

—*RYAN*
CHAPEL HILL, NORTH CAROLINA

INFORMATIONAL INTERVIEWS are always a good thing to do. You never know when people will follow up and make you an offer or ask to see you again. I didn't know if I was going to move to San Francisco, but I decided to have an informational meeting with a company just in case. Months later, I got a call from the director who told me that there was an opening. I had just figured out that I was San Francisco–bound shortly before she got in touch. It seemed so easy, and the timing was great!

—MARIANA
SAN FRANCISCO, CALIFORNIA

* * * * * * * *

SHOW CONFIDENCE. I really think that if you go into an interview knowing you're qualified for the position, you will inevitably exude that confidence, which will increase your chances.

—JIM
HOBOKEN, NEW JERSEY

* * * * * * * *

FIND OUT WHAT KIND OF SOCIAL ACTIVITIES the staff takes part in as a group. I was applying to an office that had a lot of potlucks, so I sent one of my favorite recipes in with my resume. They liked the idea (or they liked the broccoli and cheese casserole!) and I got the job.

—KARI RIDDELL
HALIFAX, NOVA SCOTIA, CANADA

* * * * * * * *

NETWORK. FOUR OUT OF FIVE INTERVIEWS that I have been granted are because I had known someone at the company or had a friend who knew someone.

—JERALYN
AUSTIN, TEXAS

FOLLOW STEPS, GET JOB

1. **Clarify your interests, skills, and goals**
   As a starting point in the job search, it is best to spend time
   identifying your interests (what you like to do), your skills
   (what you are good at doing), your values (what's important to
   you), and your personality (what qualities you possess that
   complement your other skills).

2. **Research and explore your options**
   Talking to alumni and others about what they actually do on a
   day-to-day basis can help you further identify your options and
   decide whether or not they are a good fit for you.

3. **Identify and research specific prospective employers**
   Go to career fairs, meet people through your alumni associations at school, look online at job sites like monster.com, and
   realize the importance of networking.

4. **Initiate contact, submit applications, and generate
   interviews**
   Polish your resume and cover letters. Contact the companies
   you are interested in. Request an opportunity to interview for
   information or to discuss job opportunities.

5. **Create a notebook, keep records, and follow up**
   Keep copies of cover letters and resumes you submit. Maintain
   a contact list of all prospective employers. If someone tells
   you to follow up on a certain date, make note of that date and
   be sure to follow up.

IF A JOB LOOKS LIKE IT'S NOT PERFECT, don't shoot yourself in the foot during the interview by acting like you don't care. I recently got a job for which more than 50 people were competing. The other applicants were all more qualified, with experience in the field and relevant postgraduate degrees, neither of which I have. After I was hired, my boss told me this and said the reason I was hired over everyone else was simply because they liked me and thought I had "good energy." My boss told me it seemed like the other applicants saw it as just another job, something to tide them over. The funny thing is, that's true for me, too. But I acted like I was really excited to have the chance to do the job. The job is not in my field and is not what I want to do with my life, but it turned out to be a great environment, and I'm having a great time.

> —FRED
> WASHINGTON, D.C.

Happiness is more important than success and always will be.

—KAREN
BOSTON,
MASSACHUSETTS

• • • • • • • • •

I APPLIED MY MILITARY EXPERIENCE to finding a job: Show up on time; make sure everything's crisp and polished and that you're not hungover. You've got to pay attention, get the person's card, send a thank-you, and always follow up. Good presentation has saved me when I wasn't as qualified as others. And no matter what, write notes in front of the interviewer. I do this. It doesn't matter if I'm going to use the notes; it's important for the potential employer to see that I care enough to write down what they are saying. Demeanor and attitude can count more than credentials.

> —NEIL
> TORONTO, ONTARIO, CANADA

DO NOT BE CONSTRAINED by your own expectations or anyone else's. You can always go back to a 9-to-5 job, but you might get to an age when you will feel too old to take risks and explore the world. Better to do the latter when you're young.

—*KAREN*
BOSTON, MASSACHUSETTS

• • • • • • • •

The most important thing in an interview is having fresh breath. Everything after that is gravy.

—*A.G.*
HUBBARD, OHIO

YOU HAVE TO FOLLOW YOUR HEART. This is the most important decision you will make. Don't choose a career because you think you can make bundles of money at it or because it's the career that your dad chose or because your friends think you'd be good at it. Choose the one thing you love to do and do it to the best of your ability. For me, it was teaching kindergarten. I knew that's what I wanted to do, and I have never regretted it. I know I could have made more money in other fields, but I love working with kids at that age.

—*MIA O'MALLEY*
BOARDMAN, OHIO

• • • • • • • •

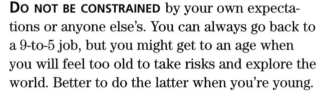

BEFORE I FIGURED OUT what I wanted to do with my life, I worked in retail for five years. Retail is a good place to find yourself. It's a nonstressful job, it will build your wardrobe and make you look sharp, and you might earn enough money to get a little independence. You can also learn practical skills; you get comfortable talking to lots of people. I also found it easy to ask customers for advice. In this role, you're always in the position of subordinate, and it's a good opportunity to ask regular customers about their lives and how they got to where they are (people love talking about themselves). You can't find this in a textbook.

—*MATTHEW WISE*
TORONTO, ONTARIO, CANADA

AFTER ARRIVING HOME FROM A JOB INTERVIEW, the first thing I do is sit down and write thank-you letters to every individual I met with during my interview. And when I say "write" a thank-you letter, notice that I did not say "e-mail" or "type" it. If you are really interested in working for them, nothing will make a better impression than the fact that you took the time to sit down and hand-write a note of thanks.

—*KENNETH C. RINEY*
DALLAS, TEXAS

• • • • • • • •

WHEN I GRADUATED COLLEGE, I wanted to be a writer. I enjoyed it, I was pretty good at it, and I hated math. But that didn't stop me from applying to be a stockbroker at one point. They gave me a test during my first interview; I remember a lot of numbers on it. I did so poorly that the guy who gave me the test thought there must have been some sort of mistake, so he offered to let me take it again. My first job out of college was in sales. After I failed at that, I waited tables, telemarketed, and worked as a greenskeeper for a country club. It was around that time that I took a tour through a CNN newsroom. I looked around and saw people my age writing and producing the news. They weren't wearing suits, and they weren't dealing with numbers. I knew it was what I wanted to do, so I got an internship at a local station and worked my way up from there.

—*J.A.*
ATLANTA, GEORGIA

WAITING TABLES IS A GREAT THING to know how to do. You can take it anywhere, get a job almost anywhere in the world, make ends meet at times in your life when things aren't going well, and always have something to fall back on. But it can also be a trap. It's likely that you can make more money waiting tables than at most entry-level jobs in the professional world. It's not a skill I would ever trade in, but I think it's important to keep your goals in mind and make sure you are always working toward them.

—*J.*
BINGHAMTON, NEW YORK

. . . .

BE CREATIVE WHEN SENDING OUT YOUR RESUME. I got a little desperate on the job hunt so I blew up my cover letter and resume to about 18 inches by 33 inches each. I made a sandwich board out of it and at the beginning of the workday, walked outside of a building that housed several shops I would have liked to work for.

—*BRANDON SMULYAN*
DALLAS, TEXAS

. . . .

BE RELENTLESS. When I decided to pursue a career, I went at it full speed. I got a list of the top 20 PR firms in San Diego and researched all of them, found the contact person and systematically called and asked for a job. From there, I just went after it and got the interviews. Persistence is key.

—*STASIA RAINES*
SAN DIEGO, CALIFORNIA

BUY SOME PLAIN BUT TASTEFUL NOTE CARDS with matching envelopes. You'll be writing a lot of bread-and-butter notes during your job hunt. And follow up. Follow up. Follow up. Your mother is not around, so you'll just have to nag yourself.

—*N.*
BROOKLYN, NEW YORK

BE BOLD. Write a letter to the top person of an organization (CEO, President, Managing Partner, etc.) and include your resume. What is the worst that can happen? That person doesn't get back in touch with you? If that person doesn't get back in touch with you, write that person a follow-up letter. If they don't respond, move on. There are too many good jobs out there to let the fear of "not getting a letter or call back" get in your way.

—*ZACH*
DALLAS, TEXAS

WHEN WRITING YOUR RESUME, see if your school/university has a career center or even an old English teacher or professor might be able to help you. Texas Tech has a career center, and I went there and got mine checked and rechecked. I also had classes where my resume was a project, so I would update it and check it through their center again.

—*MICAH KARBER*
SILVERTON, TEXAS

FIND A JOB YOU TRULY LOVE. If it's a job that you believe in and you enjoy doing, you'll work harder and want to stay longer. The temptation to call in sick or the habit of being continuously late will be obsolete if you wake up each morning thinking, "I can't wait to go to work!"

—*LACEY CONNELLY*
CHICAGO, ILLINOIS

Climbing to the Top: Do's & Don'ts in the Workforce

Y*our parents or grandparents might tell stories of a time when a person got a job out of college and stayed at that job for his or her entire career. Not only is that rare these days, it might be near impossible. The average modern worker endures/enjoys several careers in one lifetime. In other words, today's business world is constantly changing, constantly offering better opportunities, and constantly laying off or firing workers. Where do you fit in as you grab hold of the first rung on your climb?*

HAVING A GOOD ATTITUDE is more important than the quality of your work. I've seen lots of smart, talented people get fired because they consistently come in late or are rude to their boss.

—*ROBERT SALTER*
MÖNCHENGLADBACH, GERMANY

BUST YOUR ASS FOR YOUR BOSSES, WHETHER YOU WANT TO OR NOT!

—*ABBY HAGEMEIER*
LUBBOCK, TEXAS

HEAD LINES
Best Advice and Top Tips

- Do your best at any task you are assigned, no matter how small—it will lead to bigger responsibilities.

- Do more than is asked of you and your boss will notice.

- Attend work parties—but to be on your best behavior.

- Be careful about what you tell coworkers—just because you say something in confidence doesn't mean it won't get out.

- Keep a good attitude—it's as important as doing a good job.

YOU LEARN YOUR JOB by just throwing yourself into it and doing it. I was supposed to receive six months of training for a particular promotion. I had received two months of it when they told me that training was being cut short and I would be getting 10 employees at 3 p.m. I didn't know where my desk was, much less anything about my new staff. I decided to just put nametags on the 10 desks in my area and introduce myself to people as they arrived. It was nerve-racking. I made a lot of mistakes that I likely would not have made if I had been sufficiently trained. I just made the best of it.

—*JULIE MCKITRICK*
ST. LOUIS, MISSOURI

SUCK IT UP AND GO TO WORK PARTIES as much as possible. At my first job, there was a feeling that work parties were something of a requirement. I definitely went to some parties I didn't want to. But to be honest, I ended up having a good time at them, so maybe it wasn't such a bad thing.

—ANONYMOUS
BROOKLYN, NEW YORK

" It's best to play it conservative at company parties. Milk your drink; step back and observe; keep your mouth shut. I've watched four people lose their jobs because they became intoxicated. "

—JEFF CELLIO
LAGUNA NIGUEL, CALIFORNIA

YOU KNOW HOW THEY SAY you should never drink more than your boss? Well, you shouldn't bet more than him, either. When I was first getting into restaurant management, my boss took my co-workers and me to Vegas. A couple of guys started showing off, throwing around ridiculous amounts of money. When the owner saw it, he simply said, "How much do we pay our bartenders? Obviously, they're making far too much."

—T.J.K.
WESTMINSTER, CALIFORNIA

ASKING FOR A RAISE

IN MANY LARGE CORPORATIONS, the raises are given once a year—usually at the beginning of the year—on a percentage basis. You, as an employee, are given a review, and your raise percentage is based on how well you score. But I have found that if you feel you are doing a great job, you can ask for that raise to be increased or you can ask for another raise midyear. You have to be confident about your performance to do this. You don't want to get laughed out of your boss's office. But I always figured I had nothing to lose by asking.

—HILDE PARSONS
GREEN MOUNT, VIRGINIA

. . . .

YOU SHOULD EXPECT A RAISE EACH YEAR that covers inflation—3 to 5 percent. Otherwise, you're actually getting paid less for your job as time goes on. When you go in for your review, keep that in mind when you're seeking a raise—you *expect* 3 to 5 percent, and then you tack on more, depending on how well you did over the past year. A raise of 6 to 10 percent should ultimately be expected if you are doing a great job, if your employer likes your work, and if the business you're working in is doing well.

—J.A.
ATLANTA, GEORGIA

YOU MUST SEEM INTERESTED IN OTHER PEOPLE, and you must learn to listen. The young people I meet so often just want to talk about themselves and are likely to bring the conversation back to themselves no matter what the topic is. When I interview a recent graduate for a job, I look for people with emotional intelligence—someone who asks questions and retains information, not someone who wants to tell me their whole history and how their personal experiences are like my own.

—MEL MILLER
BRISBANE, AUSTRALIA

Don't try too hard; you'll look cheesy.

—ANONYMOUS
OZARK, MISSOURI

• • • • • • • •

THE HARDEST LESSON TO LEARN is that almost all jobs are terrible. Even if they seem like the dream job, there will probably be some horrible person you have to work with, or something unfair expected of you, or someone who isn't giving you credit for the things you've done. I went through at least 10 jobs before I found a job that didn't make me miserable.

—A.T.
CHAPEL HILL, NORTH CAROLINA

BIG AMBITIONS: *FORBES* MAGAZINE'S RICHEST AMERICANS

1. Bill Gates
2. Warren Buffett
3. Paul G. Allen
4. Michael Dell
5. Larry Ellison

ALWAYS LET YOUR BOSS THINK HE'S RIGHT. Mine will make mistakes and he'll scream at whomever. Everyone seems to have a problem with him, but I don't. He made me a manager and I got a raise.

—*ANNA*
WACO, TEXAS

• • • • • • • •

Always say you know how to do everything, even if you don't. Ask someone else or Google it. Bosses love competence.

—*KRISTI KAMERMAN*
BATON ROUGE, LOUISIANA

I FLIRTED WITH MY BOSS and I got the cubicle that I wanted. I was seated by people I liked. If someone gave me trouble, I didn't have to worry about it. It wasn't like I was going out with my boss. I just made friends with him.

—*K.R.*
BELLEVILLE, ILLINOIS

• • • • • • • •

GIVE YOURSELF TIME TO ADJUST to working full time. When I started, I was surprised at how exhausted I was each day when I got home. I'm an active person, but it took my body a while to get accustomed to the schedule. I've had several friends who experienced the same feeling and just wanted to sleep as soon as they got home from work.

—*ERIN BEDEL*
FOUNTAINTOWN, INDIANA

• • • • • • • •

REMEMBER THAT EVERY EXPERIENCE you have is not worthless or devoid of value, though it might seem that way at the time. So many skills and experiences are transferable to other fields of work, and often employers look for people who have a broad range of experience because they bring new, original ideas to a workplace or organization.

—*SALLY*
ADELAIDE, AUSTRALIA

HIT THE ROAD, JACK!

DON'T BE STUPID ENOUGH TO THINK THAT JUST because you tell a co-worker something in confidence, it will not get out. I made the mistake in my very first job of making a joke about my boss's hair to a guy I worked with. I hadn't been there long enough to know if I could trust him. Not only did my boss find out about what I said, he found out quickly. He called me into his office later that same day to confront me about it. He didn't fire me, but our relationship was tarnished to the point that I eventually had to quit.

—E.L.
HARRISONBURG, VIRGINIA

• • • • • • • •

IF YOU'RE A DISGRUNTLED EMPLOYEE AND DISSATISFIED with your job, you shouldn't go into work and talk about how you're ready to leave. I had one co-worker who constantly complained and even talked about what he would do in his next job and what date he thought he'd be gone by. He ended up getting let go before his planned date because management heard about all his complaining. Now I try not to gripe as much at work.

—RANDALL S. WRAY
MUNCIE, INDIANA

• • • • • • • •

MY FIRST JOB OUT OF COLLEGE WAS HELL ON EARTH. They would say, "Leanne, you need to brush your hair when you come to work." And I had brushed my hair. One day I stretched in my office and my midriff showed because my shirt came untucked. A female partner walked by right then and told me I needed to tuck in my shirt and dress more appropriately. I would cry every day. There was always screaming and yelling. They eventually let me go. But sometimes the worst thing that happens to you could be the best thing. I got another job within a few months and I've been there ever since. My boss just took us all down to the beach for a weekend. I love it.

—LEANNE
ATLANTA, GEORGIA

THREE KEYS TO SUCCESS

1. Make sure you get to work on time, meet your deadlines, and go above and beyond on any projects you are assigned. That will not only impress your boss but your co-workers as well.

2. Stay out of the office gossip; don't ever get in the middle of any personal conflicts in your work environment.

3. Always keep your cool. If something goes wrong, don't show it. People react to your reactions. If you act frazzled and stressed out, everyone around you will definitely notice, and they might start to question your abilities. You can always freak out later in the privacy of your own home.

—ASHLEY
DALLAS, TEXAS

MAKE THE MOST OF YOUR FIRST disappointing job. After going away to college, I was set on getting a job that could help save the world and keep me intellectually satisfied. I found a job as a paralegal for the number-one intellectual property law firm in the United States. I thought it would be interesting and good experience, because I had been studying law and policy in school. The first day at my job, I was shown my desk … in the basement. No windows. No sun. Only chipped beige paint and a lonely computer. I told myself it would be OK. At least I was getting paid. The firm moved to a new building four months after I started. I still work in the basement, but now most of the 40 or so other paralegals are also down there. I sit in a workroom with five others, and they are a lot of fun. My days are getting better.

—JACKIE
WASHINGTON, D.C.

KEEP UP WITH CURRENT EVENTS and trends in your industry. Managers and higher-ups at my job talk about politics and what's going on in the world. When I was in school, I mostly just concentrated on partying and studying, but now I try to stay up to date by reading CNN.com and my company's newsletter.

—RICHARD JOCO
HOUSTON, TEXAS

* * * * * * * *

" You shouldn't be in any position longer than three years. If you are, then your career is stagnating. Look at each position as a three-year task with the ultimate goal of finding a better job. "

—JOSH GRANSON
MELROSE, VIRGINIA

* * * * * * * *

CHECK YOUR WORK. And check it again. Bad things went down at my old job. I had to present some information to a union representative. I gathered it up and showed it to my manager and asked if it looked all right. She said it did, so I went ahead and presented it. But it turned out there were some big problems with it, and when everything was said and done, I actually got suspended for three days.

—SARI KEMPE
HOBOKEN, NEW JERSEY

HAIR OF THE DOG?

*W*e understand: You're a mature adult who's serious about your career. You don't have time to party like you did in college. Then along comes a Tuesday night with friends at the local pub and ... well, it seems like old times! Only now you have to rise and shine for work the next day. How will you get through it? Try these hangover cures from those who have been in your (sick) shoes.

TAKE A NAP AT LUNCH. One of the first things you should do when you start a job is find where you can take a nap if you really need one.

    —S.H.
      ATLANTA, GEORGIA

BC POWDER WASHED DOWN WITH A DIET COKE. BC Powder has aspirin and lots of caffeine in it. This, combined with the caffeine in the Diet Coke, helps a hangover. Also, as a preventative, take two ibuprofen tablets with a big glass of water prior to passing out/going to sleep!

    —KELLIE
      TAMPA, FLORIDA

THE BART SYSTEM NEVER FAILS: Bananas, Applesauce, Rice, and Toast. You'll be good as new.

    —KEITH LOBECK
      BOARDMAN, OHIO

IN THE MORNING, JUST LISTEN TO YOUR BODY. If it says, "Double Quarter Pounder with Cheese, two cigarettes, Mountain Dew, and a nap," obey. Give the hangover what it wants. This is no time to say, "We don't negotiate with terrorists."

    —J.P.
      CHARLOTTESVILLE, VIRGINIA

KNOW WHERE YOUR LOYALTIES LIE. I had been working for a company for a short time when it was announced that it was being purchased. It was frustrating because I manage eight people, and they looked to me for answers. I decided that I was going to support the company, but I was not going to lie to my employees. It was particularly tricky when one employee asked whether to pursue other work. I certainly did not want to see this person leave, but I knew that it was a good opportunity and there was a strong possibility that her job was going to be eliminated. So I told her. At the end of the day, you have to be able to look at yourself in the mirror.

> —JULIE MCKITRICK
> ST. LOUIS, MISSOURI

Have lunch with a co-worker at least once a week. When it comes time for layoffs, it helps if people in the office like you.

> —S.H.
> ATLANTA, GEORGIA

• • • • • • • •

ENGAGE IN ACTIVITIES WITH CO-WORKERS outside the office. The first place I worked, all the guys used to get together on the weekends to play flag football. I initially told them I wasn't interested, but I soon started picking up a vibe that told me that wasn't acceptable. So I gave it a try. I wanted to fit in. I hadn't played any form of football since junior high, but it came back to me pretty quickly. I found that playing football again helped me to lose some weight that I gained in college, and it was a real bonding experience with my co-workers.

> —ARIC MECHLIN
> WATTS FLATS, NEW YORK

• • • • • • • •

DO YOUR BEST AT WHATEVER TASK you're given, even if it's something you don't really enjoy. People will continue to trust you with more responsibility.

> —ERIN BEDEL
> FOUNTAINTOWN, INDIANA

DON'T BE AFRAID TO TURN DOWN a promotion if it means working for someone who will make your life miserable. I had the opportunity for a promotion that would pay a lot more per hour. I was clearly the best person for the job, but I didn't respect the person I'd be working for, so I turned it down.

—*VALERIE*
SOUTHAVEN, MISSISSIPPI

. . . .

"Everyone is faking it. No one really knows what they're doing; it's who can fake what they're doing the best. But that's OK, because the minute you think you know everything, you've stopped learning."

—*BECKY HOUK*
INDIANAPOLIS, INDIANA

. . . .

BE IN TOUCH WITH WHAT'S GOING on in the world. You'd be surprised how many conversations you can start with your boss. I had a boss who I didn't have anything in common with and didn't know anything about. Talking about the news gave me ways to stay away from the less-than-pleasing small talk.

—*JAMESE JAMES*
DALLAS, TEXAS

THE KEY TO KEEPING A JOB and advancing in the workplace is doing more than is asked of you and more than is expected of you. Work more hours than the next guy; volunteer to do the jobs that nobody wants to do; ask your boss if you can attend training seminars in your field. All that stuff is priceless. They say that water finds its own level, and it's true. But make sure your level is higher than that of the other people who work with you.

—*K.F.*
CANFIELD, OHIO

• • • • • • • •

BOSSES LIKE THE EMPLOYEE who goes the extra mile. For instance, I noticed a glitch in our company's online ordering system and I pointed it out to my boss, who then called the people above him. It turned out that no one had noticed this before. The problem was fixed, and now my boss always mentions it to me. If you see something that could help the business down the line, take the extra step. Your boss will be glad that you helped him or her look good.

—*JOSH*
WEST PLAINS, MISSOURI

• • • • • • • •

NEVER LEAVE A CURRENT JOB ON BAD TERMS, no matter how bad it is; you never know what will happen later. There were times where I was really frustrated with my job and I could've left it on bad terms. I didn't. The job I have now is because my former boss made a call. Meanwhile, my colleague left on really bad terms and can never use our last firm as a reference again.

—*JANNA*
TORONTO, ONTARIO, CANADA

You have no idea what "busy" is at this age. Don't even use the word. You don't have the right.

—*J.P.*
CHARLOTTESVILLE, VIRGINIA

I TREATED MY FIRST JOBS as if they were just like my early "jobs"—being a student. I thought that if I did exactly what was asked of me I'd get a good mark and be "promoted" to the next level. Boy, does it ever *not* work like that!

—*N.*
BROOKLYN, NEW YORK

• • • • • • • •

I HAD A BOSS ONCE WHO DIDN'T like confrontation. Instead of approaching me and telling me to my face that he might not have liked something that I did, he would send me an e-mail and copy others so everyone knew what was going on. E-mail is the wrong way to go about criticizing someone. It is embarrassing, it is impersonal, and it is a cop out. Praise, on the other hand, is something different. E-mail is one of the best ways to do it. You can e-mail them and copy their supervisors and others who will then know of that person's job well done.

—*AMY*
RALEIGH-DURHAM, NORTH CAROLINA

• • • • • • • •

DON'T FOOL AROUND WITH SOMEONE ELSE'S E-MAIL or Instant Message. One a supervisor walked away from her computer without logging out. My friend and I used Instant Message to send the coworker a message that said, "We need to make an appointment to discuss your dismissal." We thought it would be funny. It turns out, the coworker had been in trouble recently and actually thought he was being fired. He got really angry and confronted the supervisor. It was a real mess! My friend and I had to tell them what we had done. As you might imagine, they did not think it was funny. We got a note in our files.

—*CONNIE*
ST. LOUIS, MISSOURI

Back to School: Opting for Graduate Work

O nce upon a time, a bachelor's degree was enough. But with more people going to college than ever before, getting an advanced degree seems to be the new way to set yourself apart from the rat-race pack. But is grad school right for you? Whether you want to earn a higher salary in the business world, take that next step toward the Supreme Court, or just waste more time and money while improving the quality of your education, the answer is different for everyone. We surveyed college grads on the subject. Read on to decide if you need to start cramming for your entrance exams, or if you just need to find a job.

THE BIGGEST CHALLENGES of grad school are overcoming the self-doubt of living in a studio apartment at age 30 with no savings, and having to constantly answer the question, "How many more years of school do you have?"

—*KAREN*
BOSTON, MASSACHUSETTS

COLLEGE IS ABOUT FINDING YOURSELF. GRAD SCHOOL IS ABOUT FINDING A JOB.

—*D.M.*
NEW YORK, NEW YORK

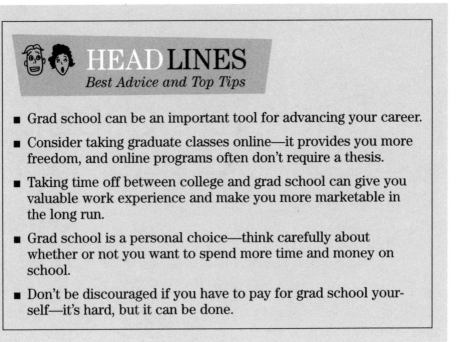

HEAD LINES
Best Advice and Top Tips

- Grad school can be an important tool for advancing your career.

- Consider taking graduate classes online—it provides you more freedom, and online programs often don't require a thesis.

- Taking time off between college and grad school can give you valuable work experience and make you more marketable in the long run.

- Grad school is a personal choice—think carefully about whether or not you want to spend more time and money on school.

- Don't be discouraged if you have to pay for grad school yourself—it's hard, but it can be done.

GO TO GRADUATE SCHOOL if your undergraduate degree is in a field where further education is extremely useful, extremely profitable, or accepted as necessary. Many of the science fields, for example, expect their graduates to continue past their undergraduate work, and the employers in those fields expect the same thing. You are not going to graduate with a degree in chemical engineering, like I did, and expect to walk into a company like DuPont and get a high-paying job. Those companies expect that they won't see you on their doorstep without at least a master's degree in hand.

—OMAR REINOR
FLORENCE, KENTUCKY

SEEK OUT EVERY PENNY and every minute you can. I eked an extra two years of working on my dissertation thanks to some really obscure fellowships. I probably put more effort into turning over every possible stone to find that money than I would have if I'd just sucked it up and worked, but it was worth it just to delay the stress of finding a real job.

> —*ELLEN*
> *KIRKLAND, WASHINGTON*

· · · · · · · ·

" Study abroad if you can. It will open your horizons. The best thing about grad school was the semester I spent in Ireland. I met my husband there, who was on a year abroad for his undergraduate program. "

> —*ANNE*
> *PARIS, FRANCE*

· · · · · · · ·

FORGET GRAD SCHOOL. Take that job at Wal-Mart and spend some time volunteering in a profession that interests you. So many young people really have no idea what is out there in the world. They just know that they need more letters behind their surname, and they make rash decisions about what those letters should be.

> —*S.G.*
> *SEATTLE, WASHINGTON*

MAKE GRAD SCHOOL A PERSONAL CHOICE. While my friends graduated college and jumped into careers, marriages, and "adult lives," I took a couple years off, stayed busy, and considered my options. I decided on medical school, applied, and was accepted. The decision never felt 100 percent right; I felt good about it slowly, week by week, month by month. Now I am graduating medical school and am really happy with my choice.

—A.F.
NEW YORK, NEW YORK

• • • • • • • •

I WENT TO GRAD SCHOOL RIGHT AWAY, and it was the best time to do it. You've already got the momentum and the discipline school requires. You have fewer obligations, financial and otherwise, at 22 versus working for 10 years and going back to school at age 32. I know if I had waited, I would have never gone back.

—JOHN BAKER
KENNEDY, NEW YORK

Follow your heart. It's the only thing that will make working in the real world bearable.

—K.R.
SAN FRANCISCO
CALIFORNIA

TOP 10 BUSINESS SCHOOLS

1. Dartmouth College (Tuck)
2. University of Michigan (Ross)
3. Carnegie Mellon University (Tepper)
4. Northwestern University (Kellogg)
5. Yale University
6. University of Pennsylvania (Wharton)
7. University of California, Berkeley (Haas)
8. Columbia University
9. University of North Carolina, Chapel Hill (Kenan-Flagler)
10. University of Southern California (Marshall)

GENERALLY SPEAKING, my grad school professors could be divided into two groups: those who worked for the university full time (code for *lack of real-world experience!*) and seemed bitter, negative, and discouraging; and those who taught a class or two each semester as adjuncts. They were awesome. These people typically had extremely successful professional careers (one had written for *Sports Illustrated* for more than 20 years) and seemed to genuinely want to help and support the students. Get to know the adjuncts early, because they'll make terrific and powerful mentors later.

—SHANNON HURD
HIGHLANDS RANCH, COLORADO

• • • • • • • •

DON'T TAKE GRAD SCHOOL FOR GRANTED. You will never again be around so many bright people. Incompetence will rear its ugly head once you hit the outside world.

—JEANIE
MINNEAPOLIS, MINNESOTA

Who the hell wants to start a life of work before they have to?

—J.G.
JAMESTOWN
NEW YORK

TOUGHEST LAW SCHOOLS TO GET INTO

1. Yale University
2. Harvard University
3. Stanford University
4. Columbia University
5. University of Pennsylvania
6. Northwestern University
7. University of California, Berkeley
8. University of Chicago
9. University of California, Los Angeles
10. University of Texas at Austin

IF YOU ARE GOING TO GO TO COLLEGE for four years, you might as well go the distance and go for one more. The additional work and money are more than made up for by the increase in earnings that a master's degree will get you. I'm a teacher, and in our union the salary increase for those with a master's degree compared to those with a bachelor's degree averages about $10,000 a year. In some fields it can be even more lucrative.

—*PERRY O'MALLEY*
HARRISONBURG, VIRGINIA

＂Take graduate classes online. I never had to set foot on a campus or deal with parking nightmares. Plus (and this is a little-known fact), for most online master's programs, you don't have to do a thesis.＂

—*S.A.*
LAKE FOREST, CALIFORNIA

IF YOU GO TO A LARGE UNIVERSITY for your undergraduate degree, do the opposite for your grad work and go to a small college. Or vice versa. You will be exposed to different ways of thinking on the same subjects.

—*LONNIE PRETNOS*
CAMPBELL, OHIO

I GOT MY DOCTORATE BECAUSE I needed to be taken seriously as a woman in a field that is very male-dominated. I would never be as financially secure and as professionally respected if I hadn't done it.

—*MEL MILLER*
BRISBANE, AUSTRALIA

• • • • • • • •

IGNORE THE PEOPLE WHO MAKE FUN of you for still being in school. My siblings kept asking things like, "When are you going to cut the umbilical cord?" It was especially hard. I finally learned to just ignore them. I figured that my parents were the ones who were supporting me, and they were fine with it.

—*JULIANA GOODWIN*
SPRINGFIELD, MISSOURI

• • • • • • • •

ANYTIME ANY OF MY FRIENDS would tell me that I was just avoiding work by staying in grad school, I'd tell them the same thing: "Yep, and you're just jealous." I think a lot of them would have done the same thing if they could have afforded it, and their comments were just sour grapes.

—*J.G.*
JAMESTOWN, NEW YORK

• • • • • • • •

YOU CAN PAY YOUR OWN WAY if you have to. My parents told me that I had to pay for my master's myself. I looked at the cost of school per credit hour. I worked 40 hours a week and saved everything I could and kept my money for school separate. On the first day, I was able to buy my books and pay in full for my first nine credit hours. That was very gratifying.

—*ANONYMOUS*
KIRKSVILLE, MISSOURI

The worst thing about grad school was looking at the under-grads and knowing how easy and fun they had it without realiz-ing it.

—*MATT*
SAN CARLOS
CALIFORNIA

GRAD SCHOOL: THREE REASONS

1. I felt like I was so much younger than everyone else in the office that I didn't get much respect.

2. Immediately after graduating from college, I realized how much of a haven school really is. I went to a small college, and I decided I wanted to see what the whole big-school-college-town thing was like.

3. Perhaps the biggest reason: I was a year removed from college, and I already felt like I was in *Office Space*. I was ready to beat a printer with a baseball bat to the tune of "Damn It Feels Good to Be a Gangsta." In sum, I decided to go to grad school out of a selfish interest in refusing to grow up and out of a search for inspiration.

    —SIMON
    GAINESVILLE, FLORIDA

I'M APPLYING TO LAW SCHOOL. Getting ready for the LSAT is like preparing for a big final. For people like myself, who have been out of school for a couple of years, there's a certain amount of mental rust to shake off before tackling a test like that. The nice part is that there are no other classes or exams to study for when you're in that situation, so the preparation is a little less frantic. It's best to sign up well in advance and give yourself a few months to get ready.

—*JESSE AMMERMAN*
CHICAGO, ILLINOIS

• • • • • • • •

IF YOU ARE HAVING TROUBLE CHOOSING between two options for a career path, consider what you want in the long run. I was having trouble during my last two years of undergraduate school deciding what to do with my life: going into medicine versus getting a Ph.D. and eventually teaching. I ended up thinking about which path would have more options in terms of lifestyle, income, and intellectual stimulation down the road. I picked medicine, thinking I would be able to choose down the line what field of medicine I wanted. It was the right decision for me.

—*R.H.*
LITTLE ROCK, ARKANSAS

• • • • • • • •

I WENT TO LAW SCHOOL AFTER TAKING a few years off. I found myself a little out of touch with many of the students who had gone straight from their undergrad to law school. In hindsight, however, it was an excellent decision because my previous work experience combined with my legal education made me very marketable in the competitive field of entertainment law.

—*ANONYMOUS*
TORONTO, ONTARIO, CANADA

Try to pick something you enjoy. If you don't enjoy what you're doing, it's going to drain your spirit and your soul.

—*WARREN*
OAKLAND
CALIFORNIA

FIT IN TRAVEL WITH YOUR FIELD OF STUDY. I did my anthropology studies in Ecuador and then stayed to work on my dissertation there, too. I was there for years and probably spent what it would've cost to be in the States for only a few months.

—*M.G.*
ALAMEDA, CALIFORNIA

• • • • • • • •

I WAITED FOR A COUPLE OF YEARS after undergrad to get my MBA. I didn't know anything about business after undergrad, so I got a job in the corporate world. I think it would be difficult to learn about business if you didn't get out and experience business first.

—*BECKY HOUK*
INDIANAPOLIS, INDIANA

• • • • • • • •

MY LAW SCHOOL ROOMMATE and I said that we were not going to get involved in that hard-nosed, competitive culture. We attended class, we studied a lot, but we did not get involved in the "who can stay at the library longest" or "I have no time to eat because I have too much to study" rituals. We continued with our normal lives and incorporated school into that lifestyle. It is possible. And it is possible to maintain good grades at the same time. The two keys are your time usage and priorities. But I can guarantee that you will be happier if you avoid the drama, headaches, and mind games of grad-school competition.

—*ZACH*
DALLAS, TEXAS

THE NEW GRE

In 2006 the GRE General test will undergo "the most significant overhaul" of its 55-year history.

CONSIDER GRAD SCHOOL CAREFULLY. I applied to med school. When I went to the interview, they told me that this would be my entire life for the next six years. They actually told me that it was a commitment more serious than marriage, that I should expect to have no life in the meantime, and that I had to be willing to want that. It was really informative. I decided it wasn't what I wanted, and my fiancée decided it's definitely not what she wanted!

—*JASON T.*
CHAPEL HILL, NORTH CAROLINA

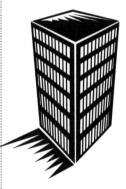

GET A GRADUATE ASSISTANT JOB within the college or with the professor/advisor you're working. This really helps you take full advantage of your degree because you are able to work with the professors to better understand and appreciate graduate school.

—*MICAH KARBER*
SILVERTON, TEXAS

TAKE ADVANTAGE OF THE EVENTS and programs available on campus. I spent a great deal of my undergraduate years focusing on my sorority and participating in social events, missing out on all the cultural and educational opportunities available on campus. Since I have been in graduate school, I have spent my free time attending lectures and plays, as well as volunteering for the Women's Center and other programs that interest me. It has been a much more rewarding experience and certainly more memorable.

—*CASEY BOND*
GRAND RAPIDS, MICHIGAN

IF YOU GO BACK TO SCHOOl after a period of "real life," you'll find that your point of view has changed. You'll be more demanding of the courses, the professors, and of yourself. You'll want to really get something of value for your time and effort, not to mention your money.

—*N.*
BROOKLYN, NEW YORK

Basic Survival Skills: Cooking, Adult Etiquette & More

S*ure, 99-cent Ramen noodles and keggers had their appeal. But unless you want to continue a college existence now that college is over, change is in order. You might want to learn how to cook a new, tasty dish. You might find yourself at a black-tie soiree. And you might want to know when and how to write a thank-you note. In this chapter, we've collected advice and anecdotes that offer the basic knowledge you need to survive a new world of expectations. Be sure you study—there will be a pop quiz.*

YOU'RE AN ADULT NOW, so dress like one. Pitch the Green Day shirt with the cigarette burn on the sleeve. Same with those jeans with the rips in the knees. Two words: cotton Dockers. As far as underwear: Start over.

—V.S.
BOARDMAN, OHIO

GET THE BIG EMILY POST ETIQUETTE BOOK. IT'S GOT TEMPLATES AND SAMPLE LETTERS.

—A.H.
BROOKLYN, NEW YORK

HEAD LINES
Best Advice and Top Tips

- Being an adult means you should dress like one.

- Send handwritten thank-yous for gifts promptly.

- When dining out keep your language and your behavior in check.

- When sending any kind of correspondence, make sure you've spelled the recipient's name correctly.

- Keep money matters private—once you're out of college it's no longer appropriate to talk about how broke you are.

WHEN I WAS IN COLLEGE, I acquired my favorite sweatshirt at a Christmas social. It is warm, heavy-duty, and forest green. On the back, though, it has a picture of Santa Claus passed out with a bottle of whiskey and a plate of cookies. I wore it with pride for four years. I've been out of school for several years, and now my wife won't let me go near the thing. I accidentally wore it to the grocery store one day, and after a few curious and disgruntled stares, my wife made me hide it away. The moral of this story is: Drunken Santa sweatshirts are only cool between the ages of 18 and 22.

—*E.E.*
ST. LOUIS, MISSOURI

IF SOMEONE CONTACTS YOU in any way—letter, e-mail, phone call, whatever—reply to them. This is how adults operate. I absolutely hate it when I call or e-mail someone and they don't get back to me.

—*C.E.*
HARRISONBURG, VIRGINIA

. . . .

" Remember everyone's name. It is the most important thing to learn in terms of etiquette. Take notes if you have to, and call people by their name every chance you get. "

—*F.R.*
BINGHAMTON, NEW YORK

. . . .

WHEN YOU GO TO A DINNER PARTY, don't bring flowers if they're not already in a vase. If somebody does this with me and I'm preparing for the dinner, I get a little frazzled. I have to figure out how to organize the arrangement, where to find a vase, and where to put the flowers.

—*ANONYMOUS*
TORONTO, ONTARIO, CANADA

. . . .

I OFTEN SEND SOMEBODY AN ARTICLE on a subject that I think would interest the person. This really shows that I paid attention to what they were saying and took the time to show I care.

—*DAVID K.*
NEW YORK, NEW YORK

BE ACCOUNTABLE FOR YOUR ACTIONS. My social life is a lot calmer. I teach dance to preschoolers, and I don't want their parents to see me out partying. I have my reputation to think of. If I go out, I might only have a drink or two and say, "OK. That's it. It's time to go home."

—MEGHAN
MASCOUTAH, ILLINOIS

• • • • • • • •

BEING AN ADULT MEANS not drinking too much at parties. It took me a little while to figure out that one, but it's important.

—AMY
DURHAM, NORTH CAROLINA

• • • • • • • •

Learn to tie a tie. Anybody who wears clip-on ties is simply a loser. You might as well wear a polyester suit.

—S.C.
HARRISONBURG, VIRGINIA

WHEN YOU'RE LEAVING SOMEONE a message on an answering machine, leave your phone number. Your friends might not care, but businesspeople get annoyed if you don't leave your contact information.

—LIZ ASHBY
EUREKA, CALIFORNIA

• • • • • • • •

WHEN I WAS GROWING UP, if I didn't write a gift note for every gift I received, my mother would beat me. Write letters. And handwrite them. You can generate those cover letters on the computer, but definitely handwrite a thank-you letter.

—LEANNE
ATLANTA, GEORGIA

• • • • • • • •

KEEP FAMILY BUSINESS PRIVATE. You especially don't talk about money. When you are in college, everybody talks about how broke they are. But it's not polite conversation in the business world.

—BETSY MILLER
MARSHFIELD, MISSOURI

WHEN YOU GET YOUR FIRST JOB and you have to dine formally for business, don't act like an uncouth slob, even if you are one. If you don't know which fork to use, there are plenty of etiquette Web sites that you can peruse. But if you get to the restaurant and you get confused, don't act flustered. Just pretend like you know what you're doing, even if you don't. It will be more noticeable to your dining companions if you stop to look around at which fork they are using than if you just pick one and go with it.

—GINA LEMKE
POLAND, OHIO

• • • • • • • •

ONCE, WHILE DINING WITH MY FRIENDS at a high-end restaurant, a waiter walked by carrying an enormous piece of cake. Without thinking, I blurted out, "Holy shit!" All I could think about was that there was no way one person could eat the whole thing! Later, my friend told me that everyone in the restaurant had turned to stare at me. When you go to a nice restaurant as an "adult," it isn't proper to talk—or curse—so loud!

—ROBIN
HARTFORD, CONNECTICUT

Until you understand how to cook, watch the Food Network for ideas.

—BRANDI
DICOSTANZO
DALLAS, TEXAS

MISS MANNERS ON THANK-YOU NOTES

"The longer you put off this task, the longer the letter you have to write. It should not contain your paltry excuses but overwhelm them with gratitude for their kindness and enthusiasm about whatever you must have long since bought with their money."

COOKING 101

In college you might have taken pride in all the out-of-the-box meals you could ingest. But life is about new experiences, and that includes learning how to cook. Here are some tips to get you started.

BY THE TIME I GRADUATED COLLEGE, I had three "quality" meals in my recipe box: taco salad, chicken stir-fry and, being from St. Louis, I could grill some of the best pork steaks. During the week, I lived on cold cuts, macaroni and cheese, and chips and salsa. But during the weekends, especially when people would come over, I would break out one of my special meals. One of my favorite memories was cooking on a little five-gallon drum a neighbor of mine had turned into a grill. I could only grill one pork steak at a time, and it took forever, but it was fun.  After a while, I learned to experiment with cooking. And now, six years later, my recipe box has about six "quality" meals in it—one for nearly every day of the week.

> —*E.E.*
> *St. Louis, Missouri*

• • • • • • • • •

I LIKE TO USE THE CROCK-POT AND MAKE A MEAL that will last for days, so I don't have to cook every night. Also, I have found that meals.com has some good recipes. My favorite source of recipes is to ask my friends because I know they will be good.

> —*Carri Jobe*
> *San Antonio, Texas*

• • • • • • • • •

PLAN OUT ALL OF YOUR MEALS AT THE START OF EACH MONTH. I actually write them on a calendar and post them on the refrigerator. My sister teases me about being so anal, but it's really helpful.

> —*Lisa*
> *Nixa, Missouri*

FANCY COOKBOOKS ARE NOT ALWAYS THE BEST. The best ones that we have purchased are these cheap "Idiot" guides to cooking. We picked up three not too long ago: one for slow-cookers, one for low-carb meals and one for five-minute appetizers.

—MATT
LITTLE ROCK, ARKANSAS

• • • • • • • • •

TRY TO EAT FRESH AND COOK FRESH. On the Internet you can find cooking recipes that are under 30 minutes. My favorite chef is Rachael Ray. There is lots of flavor in all of her meals. Enjoy creating and trying new things. Cooking is a lot of fun, especially when you share your cooking with friends.

—BRANDI DICOSTANZO
DALLAS, TEXAS

• • • • • • • • •

CASSEROLES, CASSEROLES, CASSEROLES! They are easy, are tasty, and make for great leftovers. Also, invest in those big bags of frozen, skinless chicken breasts; you can make anything with those. Bake them in the oven for 30 minutes or grill them. Cut them up for salads or just serve them with some vegetables. They are healthy and easy.

—ASHLEY
DALLAS, TEXAS

• • • • • • • • •

YOUR MEALS HAVE TO ACCOMMODATE THE PACE OF YOUR LIFE. I ate a lot of Ramen noodles in college, as well as spaghetti and frozen dinners—anything that I could make quick. Now I try to use fresh vegetables and eat healthy. But because of work and school I still like to have something quick to make. So I make a big batch of food on Sunday. I refrigerate it, and that is what I eat throughout the week.

—VERONICA
SPRINGFIELD, MISSOURI

IF IT COMES DOWN TO A CHOICE between being late and looking good or being on time and looking bad, go with the former. People will quickly forget about tardiness. However, an unseemly appearance will be remembered for a long time.

—*B.M.*
DRY RIDGE, KENTUCKY

. . . .

One time I used the salad fork to eat the whole meal. I figured I was using the right fork at least part of the time.

—*GINA LEMKE*
POLAND, OHIO

ALWAYS MAKE SURE YOU'VE SPELLED people's names correctly—in party invitations, thank-you notes, e-mails and memos at work. Nothing makes a worse impression than receiving something with your name misspelled on it. It shows a lack of respect and attention, and it essentially says, "I only halfway care about you."

—*ERIKA*
TALLAHASSEE, FLORIDA

. . . .

HERE ARE THE THINGS YOU MUST STOP doing as an adult: 1. Drinking directly out of the milk carton. 2. Forgetting to flush the toilet. 3. Leaving your underwear lying around. 4. Spending all your money on beer and cheeseburgers. 5. Sleeping until noon on days off.

—*VIGGY FAIRFIELD*
HARRISONBURG, VIRGINIA

. . . .

WHEN YOU ARE AT A FORMAL DINNER and the food is being placed on the table—particularly food that is for the table to share, like bread—never be the first to reach for it. I don't care how much anybody you ask would deny it; people always look down at the unfortunate soul who is the first to grab a roll out of the basket. Let someone else go first. Better yet, let everyone go first.

—*RALPH DILUIGI*
FLORENCE, KENTUCKY

E-MAIL ETIQUETTE

As a member of the e-generation, you certainly know how to e-mail with the best of them. But as you mature, your electronic correspondence should mature as well. Check out these tips for guidance.

- Be concise and to the point
- Answer all questions, and pre-empt further questions
- Use proper spelling, grammar and punctuation
- Make it personal
- Answer promptly
- Do not attach unnecessary files
- Do not overuse the "High Priority" option
- Do not write in CAPITALS
- Don't leave out the message thread
- Read the e-mail before you send it
- Do not overuse "Reply to All"
- Limit use of abbreviations and emoticons
- Do not forward chain letters
- Do not use e-mail to discuss confidential information
- Use a meaningful subject line
- Avoid using URGENT and IMPORTANT
- Avoid long sentences
- Don't send or forward e-mails containing libelous, defamatory, offensive, racist, or obscene remarks
- Use cc: field sparingly

If someone is older than you, call them "ma'am" or "sir." Say "please" and "thank you." You catch more bees with honey.

—*LEANNE*
ATLANTA, GEORGIA

I ALWAYS CALL SOMEONE THE NEXT DAY to thank them for inviting me to dinner or for a party. I also send thank-you cards for all gifts that same week. And in business I send thank-you cards for prospects who took the time to meet with me. It is the single most effective way I could think of to be in good standing with people: friends, clients, and family. And it feels good to acknowledge and be acknowledged—so simple, yet so powerful!

—*KALYNA*
SAN FRANCISCO, CALIFORNIA

• • • • • • • •

SINCE I'VE BEEN WORKING, LAUNDRY has taken on a whole new meaning. I have to wear nice professional clothes. That means I have to buy clothes that are either for work, or for both work and going out. It's pretty easy to find stuff that is versatile, and it saves you money if you buy a sweater or a shirt that can serve both purposes.

—*BECKY STRUBE*
BELLEVILLE, ILLINOIS

• • • • • • • •

AN INVALUABLE TOOL TO HANDLE LAUNDRY is a home-pick-up-and-delivery laundry service. I don't care if I sound like a yuppie or a suburbanite. It's worth the money and the time you save, and it's one more thing you don't have to worry about. My pick-up days are Tuesday and Friday. They pick the stuff up on Tuesday and bring it back on Friday. It is the best thing that has ever been invented.

—*AMY*
RALEIGH-DURHAM, NORTH CAROLINA

To save money, try to do dry cleaning yourself. I

Old Friends, New Friends: Making (and Keeping) Connections

T ogether forever: That's the pledge you made to your college pals as you headed off to conquer the world. And while we hope you keep your college friends for years to come (at least the ones you liked), the real world brings about real changes: new cities, new jobs, new hobbies, and yes, new friends. Sites like Friendster.com and MySpace.com have built huge networks on the idea of staying in touch with familiar faces and "clicking" with new ones. But it's still not easy to start fresh. We asked grads how they navigated a brand-new social landscape. Read on for a map that leads to satisfying friendships.

THE FRIENDS YOU HAVE in high school are your true friends. The friends you have in college are good friends. The friends you have at work are usually just acquaintances disguised as friends.

—*JACKIE EDMONDS*
  WILLIAMSTOWN, KENTUCKY

DIFFERENT PLACES EQUALS DIFFERENT PEOPLE AND NEW CONNECTIONS.

—*BRIAN*
  NEW YORK, NEW YORK

HEAD LINES
Best Advice and Top Tips

- Don't get caught up with friends who refuse to grow up—they will only hold you back.

- Make an effort to stay in touch with far-away friends—even if you only see each other once a year.

- Peruse the local papers for interesting events—they are a great place to meet people with similar interests.

- Stay active—get involved in church groups and community organizations.

- Strike up conversations wherever you go—you never know whom you'll meet.

I walk into a party or a meeting with networking on my mind.

—GEHONG WANG
ROCKVILLE,
MARYLAND

TAKE A CHANCE ON SOMEONE. I met my one very good friend, David, in the park. I was reading a book about how Judaism was like Buddhism, and he had read it, and we started talking. I'm pretty sure he was interested in me romantically; he asked me out. Sometimes you meet a guy who likes you, and you think maybe you're better off as friends. But you never know, so you go out on a date. I'm glad I did. If I hadn't gone out with David, I would have never ended up being such good friends with him. And after he introduced me to the people he knew, I suddenly found I had a whole new circle of friends.

—REBECCA SHENN
NEW YORK, NEW YORK

MY HIGH SCHOOL GIRLFRIENDS and I try to meet up somewhere at least once a year for fun weekend trips. We may not know every detail of each other's lives like we used to, but there's a strong bond and a sense of comfort when we're all together. We know we'll always be there for each other.

—*ANONYMOUS*
  SAN DIEGO, CALIFORNIA

❝ Make friends wherever you go. Friends are what keep you going through any transition. You feel more loved and more popular when you keep running into familiar faces. ❞

—*KALYNA*
  SAN FRANCISCO, CALIFORNIA

THERE ARE FRIENDSHIPS meant just for college. I was disappointed to learn that a few of the friendships I had initially deemed as everlasting fizzled out shortly after graduation. College is a time filled with fun, experimentation, life lessons, studying, achievement, and pursuit of goals. A few of my friends were perfect companions in college, but they never grew past the times of partying and financial dependence on their parents. In other words, they still have a lot of growing up to do.

—*M.H.*
  RICHMOND, INDIANA

DON'T LET YOUR PETER PAN FRIENDS, the ones who will never grow up, interfere with you moving on and getting an adult life. I had a couple of buddies who still wanted to go out and party three nights a week even after I had gotten my first accounting job. They were living at home and sponging off their parents, so it was no big deal to them. I didn't want to hurt their feelings or lose their friendship, and I didn't want them to think I was a wuss, so I continued to go out with them. But having to get up early the next day and make myself presentable for life in the office really took a toll on me. I know some days I looked less than ready to work. My boss never said anything, but I think he knew what was up. When you have adult responsibilities like a job, you have to act like an adult. Even if your friends won't.

—*A.M.*
ELLSWORTH, OHIO

• • • • • • • •

IT WAS REALLY EASY TO MEET FRIENDS in Chicago. We would go to the bars in Lincoln Park to watch basketball and football. We met a lot of people that way. I also met other young people through work and by playing volleyball at the Social Club of Chicago.

—*ANONYMOUS*
NEW YORK, NEW YORK

• • • • • • • •

MAKE SURE THAT YOU LEARN THINGS from your friends. I used to make friends without considering what they could teach me or how they could help me grow. My new friends have all have shown me complete generosity, compassion, and empathy.

—*TAI DAVIS*
PALATINE, ILLINOIS

I'VE ALWAYS HAD AN UNDERSTANDING with friends who live far away: If we lose touch, and you find yourself back home, *get in touch!* Don't feel ashamed if you haven't written or called in months or years. The longer the time spent not seeing someone, the more involved and fun it is when we finally get together. It's like when you wait forever in a restaurant and you get hungrier with every passing minute. By the time you eat, the food tastes so much better!

—ADAM SHALABY
TORONTO, ONTARIO, CANADA

. . . .

IF YOU WANT TO STAY IN TOUCH WITH PEOPLE, you have to work at it. It doesn't happen magically. I still get together once a year with a group of friends that I met in college. Every year we move the location of the reunion near a different one of us so that person does not have to pay to travel. If you can afford to do something like our annual reunion, then do it. Nothing beats seeing your old friends in person so you can see that they are aging and wrinkling just like you.

—JANE TABACHKA
GREEN MOUNT, VIRGINIA

. . . .

AFTER COLLEGE, I was living in St. Louis but worked for a consulting firm, so I was constantly placed in cities in which I didn't know anybody. At times, it was pretty lonely. I went out with people whenever I could—they didn't need to be good friends, just people from work or neighbors. This helped me meet other people in the area. I also took some classes. The experience was great because it got me out and introduced me to new people, and I learned something in the process.

—JEFF
SAN FRANCISCO, CALIFORNIA

For a party, two words: fancy cheese. Just make sure you can pronounce the type when your guests ask.

—JENNIFER
SEATTLE
WASHINGTON

OBJECT: FUN

WE'RE KNOWN FOR HAVING REALLY GREAT PARTIES with really great games, like the "No Game," when no one can say the word *no*. As the host, you just walk around casually and clip a clothespin on everyone and say, "Oh, keep on talking, don't mind me." And then when everyone has their clothespin, you say, "Keep on talking, but no one can say the word *no*, and if you get someone to say that, you get their clothespin. The first one to get five clothespins wins."

You start off by saying something like, "So, Sally, did you kill anyone on the way to the party?" And Sally might say, "Thank God, not this time." We don't want our parties to be about networking—we just want everyone to be laughing. We want people to leave the party sore from laughing so hard.

> —KAMI
> CAPE COD, MASSACHUSETTS

· · · · · · · · ·

HAVE A THEME FOR YOUR PARTY. Sometimes I'll get together with my girlfriends for a house party. One time it was a cowboy theme—the food, the attire, the music. Another time, it was about baking and "getting baked." We had a good time at that one. Themes help create a fun party atmosphere right off the bat.

> —MICHELE
> HOLLY, MICHIGAN

· · · · · · · · ·

IF A PARTY IS FEELING SORT OF LAME, there's always Twister.

> —J.A.
> ATLANTA, GEORGIA

PICK UP A NEWSPAPER and look for an interesting event or function. Consider attending as a curious observer rather than with the expectation that it must be fun or the perfect activity for you. See what you can get out of it. I even went to AA meetings just to see what it would be like. Once, I went to a circus and pretended to be working there sweeping up for a little while. You have to be creative.

—*D.S.*
  KENNEDY, NEW YORK

. . . .

" After a couple of years away from school, if a party is just the same as it was in college, that's kind of depressing. Be careful how you act. You can give off a real "Frank the Tank" vibe. "

—*JESSE AMMERMAN*
  CHICAGO, ILLINOIS

. . . .

STAY INVOLVED. In college you get really involved because there's stuff to do. When you leave college, you think there's nothing to do because your friends have moved away. But get involved with a church or community organizations. You'll be as busy as you were in college. I've got so many things I do: church, choirs, freelance writer, harpist, athletics. There's tons of stuff going on.

—*JENNIFER HUBER*
  INDIANAPOLIS, INDIANA

KEEP IN REALLY CLOSE TOUCH with one old friend, and that person can tell everyone everything. I couldn't possibly call 40 people and tell them news—that I had a car accident, or a really good gig, or whatever. If I did that, I would never get anything done and I would resent them all. Then we'd never talk.

—*KAMI*
CAPE COD, MASSACHUSETTS

. . . .

BE WARNED: You no longer live in a dorm and, sad and harsh as it may seem, not everyone may be trying to become insta-best friends with you in time for homecoming. Reserve the intimate details of your home life or love life for friends who really have earned your trust and demonstrated authentic interest (even if you have hung out a few times). Also respect other people's choice to do the same without feeling dissed.

—*T.M.*
ATLANTA, GEORGIA

. . . .

WHEN I MOVED FROM IDAHO to upstate New York, I was lonely for about the first six months. Then one day I realized that I was doing the things I liked to do—jogging, going to the movies, going to the coffeehouse, shopping, and going to the library—without ever talking to the other people at those places. It's hard to make friends if you keep to yourself. So I started striking up casual conversations with people. If someone was sitting alone at the coffeehouse, I'd go over and say hi. Same thing if I saw someone sitting alone at the movies. They didn't all turn into friendships, but a few of them did.

—*CHARLENE WHITTED*
JAMESTOWN, NEW YORK

Clean top to bottom whenever people are coming over. You actually feel better when it is done.

—*MATT*
LITTLE ROCK,
ARKANSAS

KEEP AN OPEN MIND. I have one friend that I met in a very unique way. My ex-boyfriend and I remained friends after we broke up. A few years later, I met my ex-boyfriend's live-in girlfriend, and she and I totally hit it off. It sounds odd, but it actually makes sense to click with your ex's partner: You probably have a lot of the same qualities.

—*JENIFER MANN*
CASTRO VALLEY, CALIFORNIA

• • • • • • • •

AT FIRST, THE MAIN DIFFERENCE between parties before and after college was that you didn't have to pay for a cup at the door. Now, I attend dinner parties and enjoy myself much more with a small group. We laugh, talk, eat, drink, and there's a lot less puking the morning after. It still happens sometimes, but not *every* time.

—*ANONYMOUS*
SAN DIEGO, CALIFORNIA

• • • • • • • •

LATELY I ONLY MAKE FRIENDS when I feel a strong and organic connection. The new relationships I've entered have been natural. I haven't had to make too much of an effort to solidify the friendship.

—*NICHOLAS WEISS*
SAN FRANCISCO, CALIFORNIA

• • • • • • • •

I SOUGHT OUT NEW FRIENDS by joining groups like Junior League, which is dedicated to training women volunteers. I also got involved in our church. Volunteering for a cause that you care about is great because you automatically share a common interest.

—*ALISON BRAWNER*
SPRINGFIELD, MISSOURI

E-GENERATION

Nearly 100 percent of college grads send and receive e-mails daily and expect e-mail to be a primary means of contact among their friends.

I PLAY TENNIS AND BASKETBALL. It's a great way to meet friends and get exercise. It's also a good way to get a date; you automatically have something in common. I find that people who play tennis are usually passionate about the sport, and I am drawn to passionate people.

—JAMES
NEW YORK, NEW YORK

• • • • • • • •

IF YOU DECIDE TO STAY IN A SMALL TOWN, be nice to everyone. There's always going to be that person who drives you crazy, but you still gotta be nice. In a small town, if you pollute your environment with even one enemy, it can make your life miserable.

—ANONYMOUS
CHAPEL HILL, NORTH CAROLINA

• • • • • • • •

U USE EVITE?

Launched in 1998, evite.com helps promote an average of 200,000 events per month.

WHEN MEETING PEOPLE, it's your outgoingness and daily activities that matter, no matter your location. If you went to the gym every day in your old city, and you met a bunch of people there, then chances are you're going to work out in your new city, too, and you'll find friends at that gym.

—JEFF CELLIO
LAGUNA NIGUEL, CALIFORNIA

• • • • • • • •

TO HANG OUT WITH OLD FRIENDS and make new ones, have a party at your house or apartment. Invite everyone you know through evite.com and encourage them to bring a friend or two. All you need after that are drinks, music, and some food. You'll hang with your good friends and meet new ones. Parties are the best way to socialize—much better than being at a bar.

—J.A.
ATLANTA, GEORGIA

INGREDIENTS FOR A GROWN-UP PARTY

When having your first adult party, make something that actually involves a recipe, instead of soup mix and sour cream or jarred cheese in the microwave. You can still rely on good old chips and salsa, but also try a more complicated hors d'oeuvre, a multi-ingredient dip or a dessert that doesn't come out of a box. If you expect people to bring something, say so (a polite way to do this is to say, "Bring something to share"), but have a base of drinks (a 12-pack of beer, a bottle of vodka) and food on hand. Make sure you have either bought ice or made a bunch of it ahead of time. Have plenty of mixers available (ginger ale, some kind of cranberry juice, a citrus-based juice, and Coke are good basics).

Clean out your fridge. Clean the bathroom (yes, the bathtub too—someone will inevitably look in there) and empty *all* wastebaskets. Have a container set aside for bottles and recycling. Make sure a bottle opener is handy. Cut up some limes and put them in a bowl near the bottle opener. Empty the dishwasher.

Light some candles. Make a CD mix or put everything on shuffle so you're not jumping up and down to change discs all the time. Introduce all your guests to each other. Remember you are the host, not the life of the party, but have good conversation tidbits ready (movie trivia, news items, good news about a common friend) for awkward moments. Offer to refill drinks; don't rely on guests to simply help themselves. And save the rubber Nixon mask and the piñata for Halloween.

—*T.M.*
ATLANTA, GEORGIA

DON'T EXPECT YOUR FRIENDS TO BE PERFECT. My best friend got really jealous when I started hanging out with other people. To retaliate, he started saying nasty things behind my back. Instead of whining about it, I confronted him, and we resolved the situation like adults. Accepting people's imperfections is part of growing up.

—D.S.
DENVER, COLORADO

• • • • • • • •

" I strike up conversations everywhere. You never know who you'll meet. The other night I met a nice couple sitting at the bar. We ended up having a great time and exchanged numbers. "

—ROBIN VELLIS
CLARKS SUMMIT, PENNSYLVANIA

• • • • • • • •

WHEN YOU'RE ON YOUR OWN, you discover things about yourself. I've realized that I can survive on my own—no parents, no boyfriend. Just me and a restaurant job and a tiny studio apartment in the city. This place is crawling with people like me, and making friends is effortless. I've also learned how fluidly people enter and exit my life, stopping momentarily and then passing by. I expect a lot more of this to come.

—JESSICA
SEATTLE, WASHINGTON

TAKE TIME TO DEVELOP YOUR HOBBIES, your creativity, and your spirit. I stopped trying to meet people and followed my passions—writing, art, and music—and the people just showed up in the strangest of ways. Finding my passion was the best way to meet new people.

—MARK LINDEN O'MEARA
VANCOUVER, BRITISH COLUMBIA, CANADA

• • • • • • • •

AFTER GRADUATING COLLEGE, my boyfriend and I broke up because our lives seemed to be heading in different directions. That summer my best friend and I made lofty, often vague plans on how to get away from home and start living in the "real" world. About three-quarters of the way through the summer, my boyfriend and I decided to get back together and try to work life out together. We decided that my best friend couldn't live with us; we were ready for domesticity, and she was going to be a third wheel. When I told her our decision, she was hurt and didn't speak to me for weeks. Making that decision was tough because I know she was afraid of being alone, and I had to let her down by choosing to live with someone else. It's tough, but in the end our friendship is stronger.

—JACKIE
WASHINGTON, D.C.

For a dinner party, keep it simple— dessert and wine. Cheap, but elegant.

—CARRI JOBE
SAN ANTONIO
TEXAS

Be active. Club Med and adventure sports are good ways to make connections.

—*WARREN*
OAKLAND
CALIFORNIA

WHEN THROWING YOUR FIRST ADULT PARTY, you are most likely going to have to stay within a tight budget. At times like this, Wal-Mart and Target are your best friends. You can throw an excellent "adult-looking" party for under $100 (depending on the size of the guest list). Wal-Mart or your local grocery store usually has a great selection of finger foods, beverages, and sweets. Target can supply all of your decorations, napkins, and plates. For background music, burn some of your favorite party songs to a CD.

—*ASHLEY*
DALLAS, TEXAS

• • • • • • • •

IF YOU DECIDE TO MOVE in with the opposite sex (just as friends) make sure you know what you're getting yourself into. I had roommates all through college, and not once did I have a problem with any of them. I moved in with a girl, and it was the hardest thing to deal with in my life.

—*BRANDON*
DALLAS, TEXAS

• • • • • • • •

I KNEW I WAS TRULY ON MY OWN the first time I got a bad case of flu after moving into my own apartment: Mom wasn't there to bring me hot soup on a tray, smooth the sheets, and put my hair up in a ponytail. Eventually, a friend of mine dashed over on his lunch hour with a can of Campbell's Chicken Noodle Soup and a can opener. Without even taking off his coat, he plopped the soup into a pan, heated it up, poured it into a bowl, handed me the bowl and a spoon, and rushed back to work. I was so grateful!

—*N.*
BROOKLYN, NEW YORK

DON'T TRY TO BE PERFECT. Let everything hang out. You'll be surprised to find that people will want to help you. If you tell them what's going on with your life, what challenges you are encountering, people are more willing to help you and brainstorm ideas. And you get closer to people that way.

—*BRODIE*
SITKA, ALASKA

• • • • • • • •

ALWAYS MAKE NEW FRIENDS; you never know when the old ones are going to head in a different direction. When I first moved to a big city out of college, I went there with my best friend. But after a short period of time, she went back home and I was left alone. I had no choice but to make new friends.

—*MICHELE*
HOLLY, MICHIGAN

• • • • • • • •

DON'T SEND MASS E-MAILS TO YOUR FRIENDS. It's impersonal. Some of my friends will write a huge e-mail about what's going on in their lives and then send it to something like 20 people. When I read them, I realize I'm usually like 10th on the list. So what am I supposed to do? Am I supposed to write them something back that's specific to them? Or should I send a generic response and address it to 20 other people?

—*BECKY STRUBE*
BELLEVILLE, ILLINOIS

NEW FRIENDS BECOME OLD FRIENDS faster than you might think.

—*N.*
BROOKLYN, NEW YORK

• • • • • • • • •

SEEK THE PEOPLE YOU have something in common with. Adult friendships are segmented. The married people group together, the parents group together, the single people group together. It's just because you have more in common. We all evolve and want to talk about what's big in our lives.

—*BECKY HOUK*
INDIANAPOLIS, INDIANA

Looking For Love: Romance (and Loneliness) After College

After college, everything changes in the world of dating. Even if you don't feel ready for marriage, there seems to be more emphasis placed on the romantic future of your dates. Another change: Unlike college, there aren't scheduled events every weekend to help you mingle with dating prospects. In the real world, you've got to find Mr. or Mrs. Right on your own. We asked college grads to give advice on the differences between college and postgrad dating, the search for love (or just a one-night stand), the downsides of dating coworkers, and how to battle loneliness when the e-mail box is empty and the cell phone is silent.

THE MAIN THING THAT'S DIFFERENT for me and dating is that my opening line—"So, are you in a sorority?"—no longer works.

—*DANE GOLDEN*
SAN FRANCISCO, CALIFORNIA

YOU DON'T FIND LOVE; IT FINDS YOU.

—*ANONYMOUS*
SAN DIEGO, CALIFORNIA

HEAD LINES
Best Advice and Top Tips

- Once you leave school you have to really put yourself out there to meet new people.
- Use your 20s as a time to date all kinds of people before you settle down.
- Don't rush into a serious relationship—spend some time getting to know yourself first.
- Dating coworkers is asking for trouble.
- Don't linger in a relationship if you know it's not working.

FOR BOTH GUYS AND GIRLS, dating in college is too easy. Everybody is forced to hang out, whether through classes or other groups. It's like shooting fish in a barrel. Real-world dating is more like deep-sea fishing: You need to put yourself out there farther and cast a strong line.

—*JESSE AMMERMAN*
CHICAGO, ILLINOIS

• • • • • • • •

PERSON-TO-PERSON CONTACT IS NECESSARY. Online dating in this MySpace era just pushes people further apart. Cell phones and instant messaging are a far second to actually being with people face to face.

—*LOUIS HAGMAN*
SEATTLE, WASHINGTON

Guys, if you are living alone in an apartment, try to keep it in decent shape. I'm not suggesting you have to vacuum and wash the windows daily, but you have to at least pick up after yourself. About six months after I got my own place, I brought this girl home from a night at the bar. We were getting comfy on the couch, and all was going well until she accidentally slid her hand between the cushion and the couch and touched a piece of week-old, half-eaten pizza. What a mood killer! After that, I became much more cleaning-conscious.

—*B.C.*
Harrisonburg, Virginia

• • • • • • • •

Is it OK to date someone you work with?
There are two rules, and a logical corollary:

1. Never date your bartender.

2. Never date someone you work with.

3. Corollary (because two negatives make a positive): You can date your bartender if you work with her. The idea is that the soap opera is part of the fun of working in a bar.

—*Daren*
Decatur, Georgia

Get a cell phone. And don't make your outgoing message juvenile. That's a sure way to turn off dates.

—*A.J.*
San Francisco, California

COLD FEET?

In 1950, the average age at which men got married was 22.8; for women, it was 20.3. Half a century later, the average age for men is 26.8, and for women it's 25.1.

TAKE THE TIME WHEN YOU'RE YOUNG (early 20s!) to date all kinds of people so you don't feel as curious later on. I went out with someone right after college for seven years. Now, at 30 years old, I'm eager to experience different men before I get married.

—*A.C.*
TORONTO, ONTARIO, CANADA

DON'T BE TOO QUICK TO FALL IN LOVE. It's a mistake a lot of people make, maybe because being out of school makes them insecure and they want something to hold on to, or maybe because they think it's part of being grown-up. I fell in love with someone. But I also eventually felt like I was missing out on freedom, on dating, on living my life without having to think of the implications for someone else.

—*F.S.*
CHAPEL HILL, NORTH CAROLINA

DATE PEOPLE YOU'VE SEEN in other relationships, because you learn how they act toward their significant other. After all the different boyfriends I've had in the past few years, it's funny that I ended up with one of my very best friends.

—*CHERI RIOT*
MISSION VIEJO, CALIFORNIA

THE FINER THINGS

"Physical attraction has its limitations. At some point it wears off, so [people] must educate themselves about art and music and food. That is what remains. As long as you breathe art at every moment, you understand the world."

—*ROBERTO CAVALLI, DESIGNER*

THROW THOSE FLANNEL PAJAMA PANTS AWAY! You *never* know where you'll meet a significant other or even (drum roll, please) Mr. or Mrs. Right. One of my best friends met her fiancé while at a convenience store. Do you think her fiancé would have approached her if she had on her favorite flannel pants with socks and sandals? I don't think so.

> —*JAMESE JAMES*
> *DALLAS, TEXAS*

• • • • • • • •

" People aren't going to knock on your door and ask to be your date. Put yourself out there. If I think a guy is cute, I talk to him. What do I have to lose? He'll say, 'You're stupid.' And I'll say, 'So are you.' "

> —*LEANNE*
> *ATLANTA, GEORGIA*

• • • • • • • •

IF YOU KNOW IT'S NOT WORKING, get out immediately. Once, a guy asked me out to dinner and the waitress took a long time to take our order, so he and I started to talk. We quickly realized we had *nothing* in common. So I said, "You know, it's really early. If we go now, we still have time to meet someone else." It was great: We both parted ways and we were both clearly relieved.

> —*KELLY JUSTICE*
> *RICHMOND, VIRGINIA*

ANY YOUNG WOMAN who has a college sweetheart should give the relationship some time in the real world before committing to a marriage. The old-fashioned tradition of marrying young and not experiencing life on your own is just not good for women—or men, for that matter. A relationship can be wonderful in college, but that doesn't always translate once you're out in the real world.

—*G.H.*
CHAPEL HILL, NORTH CAROLINA

* * * * * * * * *

100 MILLION

That's the number of single Americans. This group comprises 44 percent of all U.S. residents age 15 and over.

YOU HAVE TO BE COMFORTABLE with yourself and realize that sometimes it's better to be alone. There were a lot more men to choose from in college, so when things started going bad with one guy, there was always someone else waiting. After college, it was harder to meet available guys. The older I got, the more "taken" men I met. So when things went bad with one guy, the alternative was being alone. For someone who dated constantly through high school and college like I did, being alone was a hard thing to really get comfortable with. But every woman should have her alone time before committing to marriage and family.

—*ANONYMOUS*
SAN DIEGO, CALIFORNIA

* * * * * * * * *

TAKE TIME TO GET TO KNOW YOURSELF. During school, dating was instigated by substantial amounts of alcohol. Most of us wouldn't be getting together in school without those circumstances! After college, I didn't date for a very long time, as I was focused on other things. I haven't regretted that.

—*DARCY BELANGER*
SHERWOOD PARK, ALBERTA, CANADA

GUYS, A GOOD QUESTION to ask your date early on is, "What do you think about kids?" If the girl says anything other than, "I'd like to run them over with my Harley Davidson," I'd suggest you get your butt out of there.

> —B.P.
> FRANKFORT, KENTUCKY

• • • • • • • •

I PLAY SOFTBALL AND IT'S A GREAT WAY to meet people, mostly because there's no pretension there. People who play are generally out to have a good time. I've had a few dates that have come out of playing ball.

> —LYNETTE
> ST. LOUIS, MISSOURI

• • • • • • • •

TAKE THE TIME TO PLAN OUT A DATE. If someone has agreed to go out with you, you should do them the courtesy of planning the evening: where you're going to go, what you're going to do.

> —ANONYMOUS
> LOS ANGELES, CALIFORNIA

✓

Late-late nights! Random hookups! Forgotten phone numbers! There's something magical about dating in your early 20s.

> —J.A.
> ATLANTA, GEORGIA

FORBES MAGAZINE'S BEST CITIES FOR SINGLES

1. Denver
2. Washington/Baltimore
3. Austin
4. Atlanta
5. Boston
6. Los Angeles
7. Phoenix
8. New York
9. San Francisco/Oakland

THE DOWNSIDE OF INTER-OFFICE DATING

DO NOT HAVE SEX WITH YOUR COWORKERS. This should be printed on every page of this book. *Do not have sex with your coworkers.* Well, unless you are about to get fired. Then bang away.

—*S.H.*
ATLANTA, GEORGIA

• • • • • • • •

ONCE YOU'RE OUT OF COLLEGE, pretty much anybody is fair game—except coworkers. I've dated a few different colleagues, and all those relationships have done is cause trouble. Normally you go to work to escape a fight, but when you have to see that person there, too, you have nowhere to hide. It ultimately affects your performance because, unfortunately, you can't break up with work.

—*T.J.K.*
WESTMINSTER, CALIFORNIA

• • • • • • • •

I LEFT A JOB I REALLY LIKED BECAUSE of an office relationship that turned ugly. I had been dating this coworker, and it turned out he was engaged to someone else. I found out when I heard his friends talking about it in the elevator. He got married, and he became very bizarre with me—breaking into my computer and coming to my house. My boss and a lot of other people got involved, and it just got to a point where I wanted it all to go away. A job opened up somewhere else, so I decided to take it.

—*BETH*
SHAKOPEE, MINNESOTA

WHEN DATING IN THE WORKPLACE, you have to be a lot more sensitive than you were in the dorms. A lot of places I worked had a "one proposal" rule: If you ask someone out and get shot down, don't bug them again. That's a good rule.

—*ANONYMOUS*
LOS ANGELES, CALIFORNIA

COLLEGE AMOUNTS TO A FOUR-YEAR DATING SERVICE, with potential mates lurking (sometimes literally) around every corner. Once that's over, the options narrow drastically. For many of us, that means coworkers. When you put guys and girls in the same building for any extended period, a few are bound to copulate with each other. It's a situation rife with peril. Sometimes it works. When it doesn't, you just get back to work, clean up the graffiti that's now on your office desk, and move on.

—*JESSE AMMERMAN*
CHICAGO, ILLINOIS

I MET MY CURRENT WIFE at a book convention. She was at a party and we had a lot in common. She was in marketing and I was in promotion.

Meeting in a natural setting was the best way to connect. There was no pressure to think of what would happen after the conference, and I never imagined it would've developed into a wonderful marriage. I'm very thankful we were both working that weekend!

—*BRIAN F.*
WESTCHESTER COUNTY, NEW YORK

"Watching how the house-mates on MTV's *The Real World* hook up is not the way people hook up in the *real* real world. In fact, there is very little real-world reality on *The Real World.*"

—*CATHY HOPKINS*
COVINGTON, KENTUCKY

JUST PICK UP THE PHONE AND CALL HOME. My family was always happy to hear from me, especially my mom. And if she ever suspected that I was calling because I was lonely, she never let on. Come to think of it, I'm sure she knew. Don't moms always know?

—*GERALD PERRY*
INDEPENDENCE, KENTUCKY

DON'T DATE ANYONE WHO LIVES in the same apartment building as you do. That will just cause you both to be uncomfortable after the breakup. I went out with this one guy three or four times, and then I broke it off. He didn't take it too well. Because he knew where I lived, it was hard to avoid him. I was always sitting in my place in the dark so he wouldn't know I was home. Then I always had to look out the window to make sure he wasn't out there before I left. Luckily for me, he moved out about six months after our breakup. But it was a long six months for me.

—*MARYBETH COFNOR*
YOUNGSTOWN, OHIO

• • • • • • • •

HAVE FUN! During college, I was in a long relationship that I came out of in senior year. Through the years following, I realized I had freedom and a lack of consequences to casual encounters. So I had a few more of those.

—*MATT STONE*
SAN FRANCISCO, CALIFORNIA

• • • • • • • •

IT WAS MEN THAT were the big distraction in my early 20s, and men that always tripped me up. Young men are all so horrible. I wish I had completely ignored them until I was into my 40s.

—*MEL MILLER*
BRISBANE, AUSTRALIA

• • • • • • • •

TO FIGHT LONELINESS, STAY BUSY. I took a volunteer teaching job. I joined a men's soccer league. I work out five times a week, and I go to bars and strike up conversations. You just have to be willing to go out and talk to people.

—*DANIEL*
YORKTOWN, NEW YORK

How could you be lonely? At that stage of your life, the world is your playground. Get out there and do something!

—*B.P.*
FRANKFORT,
KENTUCKY

SPENDING TIME ALONE is not the end of the world. Young people today are used to so much visual and audio stimulation from their Game Boys and PlayStations and cell phones that when it's just them and the four walls of their apartment, they don't know what to do with themselves. You should look at that quiet alone time as time to think and plan and reflect. You'll get to know yourself much better and understand who you are and where you are headed. Stop and listen to the little voice inside once in a while.

—*R.D.*
KEEZLETOWN, VIRGINIA

• • • • • • • •

" Do not ever assume it is the other person's responsibility to handle contraceptives, disease protection, or extra lube. Better to have too much than none, right? "

—*T.M.*
ATLANTA, GEORGIA

• • • • • • • •

IT'S OK TO TAKE TIME BETWEEN RELATIONSHIPS. Try to understand your emotional triggers during this time; allow yourself time to breathe, but don't hold back if somebody special comes along. I did this recently, and it's made my current relationship a lot deeper.

—*MARK LINDEN O'MEARA*
VANCOUVER, BRITISH COLUMBIA, CANADA

TO LIVE TOGETHER?

I had a few boyfriends after I graduated college. At 25 years old, I met a man I would later move across the country to be with. We lived together for five years. It was a huge growing experience. I loved living with my ex. But when you're living with someone, you get all the dirt of a marriage (dirty socks on the floor, a sex life you have to work at, and so on) but not all of the rewards. Some of the rewards are discussing your shared goals, visions, and dreams. Living together is a strange in-between place where you're still assessing if you want to spend your life with your partner.

Don't fool yourself into thinking living together is a necessary step. If you've been dating a while, chances are you've slept over at your boyfriend's or girlfriend's place, and you've had a window into their living habits. Many people who happily marry have not taken this step and have learned to adjust and live with the person they love.

—ANONYMOUS
TORONTO, ONTARIO, CANADA

Always follow your heart. It is never OK to settle. If you settle, you'll end up miserable.

—*HEATHER POLLOCK*
ORANGE COUNTY,
CALIFORNIA

THE DANGEROUS THING IS TO FALL IN with people that you wouldn't usually have anything to do with, just because you want friends or love. Right after college, I fell in with this boy who was not good for me, and I think it was because of loneliness. I desperately wanted to connect with someone, have a routine, and share my experiences. I wish I could have turned that experience into an opportunity to appreciate myself, get to know myself, learn to be a friend to myself.

—*E.F.*
HARTFORD, CONNECTICUT

● ● ● ● ● ● ● ●

"HE'S SEEN ME NAKED! YIKES!!!" If you don't want to think that about your boss, don't date at work, unless you think you could marry that person. It can make things very awkward in the office. Even if you justify it with, "But he is in a different department; it won't make a difference," just say no. I dated a guy for a couple of months while I was a temp at a company. I thought that it wouldn't matter. Then I got a permanent job at that company and still thought it was OK because he worked on the opposite end of the building. He ended up switching departments and got a promotion and ended up being my boss. Very awkward situation, especially when review time came around.

—*JERALYN*
AUSTIN, TEXAS

● ● ● ● ● ● ● ●

EVERY YEAR, when August rolls around, I seem to get really lonely. I start thinking about all the good times my friends and I had in college. I call them and reminisce about old times. That seems to take care of it ... until next August!

—*LIBBY WARD*
SPRINGFIELD, MISSOURI

I THINK YOUNG PEOPLE confuse loneliness with boredom. Here's the difference: If you feel like you need to talk to someone face to face or on the phone, that's loneliness; if you feel like you need to get out of the apartment and do something, whether or not anybody is available to do it with you, that's boredom. Loneliness can always be cured by picking up the phone. There is always someone to talk to. Boredom is trickier, because sometimes you have to find some money to cure that.

> —CAM THORNTON
> JAMESTOWN, NEW YORK

. . . .

" I found that if you keep a steady stream of girls coming in and out of your life, you never seem to get lonely. And your bathroom will always miraculously get cleaned. "

> —J. BERNARD
> CANFIELD, OHIO

. . . .

FIND A NEW HOBBY. The minute I finished college, I had so much time on my hands I took up knitting. I'm not good enough at it yet for it to be relaxing, but I did make a little "bunny monster" for my iPod.

> —DESIRE'E MARTINEZ
> SAN ANTONIO, TEXAS

I FOUND THAT I FELT LONELY whenever things in my life were moving fast. You need to slow down and be more attentive to yourself and your surroundings. This can begin by eating more conscientiously, making healthier choices, and taking time to enjoy your food. It might also mean scheduling regular walks or bike rides and stopping to notice some interesting shop or garden along the way. A fast-paced life definitely contributes to feelings of being alone.

—*D.S.*
KENNEDY, NEW YORK

Red Alert: Cars, Credit Cards & Other Money Matters

*F*ew experiences say "real world" like balancing your own check-book. Now that you're paying your own bills, it can be disheartening to see how quickly the cash goes. There are those student loans to pay off, cool clothes to buy, and rent to pay. It would be great if you could dump that old junker for some new wheels. Can you afford to do all this and still have money for Friday nights with friends? Before you head down the road to Chapter 11 (bankruptcy, not the next section of this book), read on for financial advice you can't afford to pass up.

I'VE HAD MORE FUN and more luck when I haven't planned for things. Except in financial matters. It's too stressful not to have a plan with your money.

—MICHAEL ALBERT PAOLI
TORONTO, ONTARIO, CANADA

BUY THE CHEAP BRAND OF EVERY-THING.

—WENDY
ALLENTOWN
PENNSYLVANIA

HEAD LINES
Best Advice and Top Tips

- When buying a car, get pre-approved for financing from your bank—you'll get a better interest rate than if you finance through the dealer.
- Set a monthly budget and stick to it.
- Pay more than the minimum on your credit cards.
- Try to use credit cards only for emergencies.
- Keep enough money in your savings account to cover at least one month's expenses.

PAY OFF YOUR STUDENT DEBT and any loans with higher interest rates as soon as possible. I recently inherited money from my family and wrote a check for $20,000 toward my student loan debt. It felt really good and really odd to write a check for that amount!

—*RANAI*
SAN FRANCISCO, CALIFORNIA

· · · · · · · ·

SINCE I DON'T HAVE AN ACTUAL RETIREMENT account, and since Social Security may not exist in 40 years, my current approach to retirement planning is a little thing I call the state lotto.

—*JESSE AMMERMAN*
IOWA CITY, IOWA

I GOT A CREDIT CARD THAT has no annual fee and an awards program. For every dollar I spend, I earn one point. Points can be redeemed for anything: cash, gift certificates, travel. Every time I charge something (and I charge everything I can), I automatically deduct that amount from my check register. That way, when the bill comes, I know I have enough money to pay it in full. Doing this, I've managed to build up enough points in a year to earn a free airline ticket. Plus, I have no debt and an excellent credit rating.

—*SHANNON HURD*
HIGHLANDS RANCH, COLORADO

MOST BANKS WILL REFUSE TO FINANCE you for more money than a new car is actually worth. So, if your bank turns down your loan request even though you have great credit, but the dealer is saying, "Oh, we'll make it work if you finance through us!" this is a huge red flag. This happened to me, but, at the time, I was too naive to know what it meant. I wanted the car so badly that I accepted the dealer's financing offer and ended up paying the sticker price of $16,000. Unfortunately, I found out a couple of weeks later that the car was only worth about $8,000.

—*R.W.*
FORT COLLINS, COLORADO

BUYING THOSE BOOTS BEFORE YOUR TRIP to New York City is ***not*** an emergency!

—*MICHELE*
HOLLY, MICHIGAN

I'VE LEARNED THAT NOBODY IS TOO GOOD to go out and flip burgers. When I was trying to start my own business, I did whatever I could to make money. I was determined not to ask my parents for money, even though I know they would have gladly helped. If you want to be an adult, you have to learn to make it on your own.

—*BETSY MILLER*
MARSHFIELD, MISSOURI

· · · · · · · ·

WITH CAR INSURANCE, don't get anything except liability insurance. Everything else is a scam. I only pay about $200 every six months for car insurance. Think about it: If you look at your lifetime, how many car wrecks do you actually have? The full coverage doesn't pay for itself.

—*RICH*
ANN ARBOR, MICHIGAN

· · · · · · · ·

WHEN BUYING CAR INSURANCE, shop around. You can check quotes on the Internet for just about every company out there. Or you can call them. I just changed my coverage about a year ago, and I'm now paying about $300 less a year than I was for the exact same coverage. That would probably pay for one Saturday night at a strip club.

—*SHEILA MANNING*
KEEZLETOWN, VIRGINIA

· · · · · · · ·

WHEN DOING YOUR TAXES FOR THE FIRST TIME, do it on paper, not electronically. Use Form 1040EZ or Form 1040A. Those are the easiest tax forms to fill out. They are very user-friendly. I felt very comfortable the next year after getting through that first time.

—*A.D.*
HARRISONBURG, VIRGINIA

THE RIGHT FOOT?

The average college graduate owes nearly $20,000 in student loans.

TO SAVE YOURSELF SOME CASH, you have to learn to do some stuff on your car. Nothing major. But if you can change your oil and your wiper blades and burnt-out lights and even your brakes, you can really save compared to going to a garage for all that stuff. If you don't know how to do it, experiment. You're smart; you'll figure it out.

—*MELANIE SPLANE*
YOUNGSTOWN, OHIO

• • • • • • • •

" As soon as I got my first job, I went credit-card crazy. It's so easy to do. Shoes were my weakness. I eventually got in so deep that I had to cut the card up to keep myself from using it. I was like an addict. "

—*LEAH GERSON*
ZIRKLE, VIRGINIA

• • • • • • • •

GET FINANCED THROUGH YOUR BANK FIRST so you can walk into the dealership with a check. It's like paying cash, which gives you a lot more negotiating power. Plus, it's cheaper because dealerships try to screw you with their financing. My husband and I got an interest rate of 3.9 percent through our credit union. The dealership, on the other hand, was going to charge us much more.

—*S.A.*
LAKE FOREST, CALIFORNIA

TO DIVERT MY ATTENTION AWAY from the overall price of the car, my salesperson kept asking me over and over what monthly payment I could afford. He got me so focused on lowering my payment that I didn't even realize I was being suckered into paying $30,000 for a car that's worth about $20,000. Watch out for this tactic!

—*D.S.*
DENVER, COLORADO

Pay down more than your minimums! I wish I did that more.

—*KALYNA*
SAN FRANCISCO, CALIFORNIA

• • • • • • • •

I BOUGHT MY MOST RECENT CAR from a broker. Car brokers do everything for you: You tell them exactly what you what in terms of make, model, year, condition, and price, and they go out and find it. They have access to cars that are going up for auction, and cars whose leases have just expired, so they can find you a really good deal. They will even negotiate the car loan, take care of registration, and deliver your vehicle to you. I know they probably tacked on a fee to the overall price, but I didn't care. The bottom line is I ended up with exactly the car I wanted, did no legwork, and still paid less than I would have if I'd gone to a dealer.

—*SAJIT GREENE*
UTICA, NEW YORK

• • • • • • • •

WITH MY FIRST JOB, I made the mistake of not having enough federal tax withheld from my pay. When it was tax time, I didn't have the money to pay my taxes and had to borrow from my parents. I was so embarrassed. You probably won't be making a fortune with your first job, so be sure to have extra money withheld. If you don't see it, you won't miss it, and it can make things easier for you come April 15.

—*MINDY HILDENBRAND*
HARRISONBURG, VIRGINIA

I WANTED A CAR that reflected professionalism, and I ended up leasing. You can get into leasing with a lower monthly payment than purchasing. You don't have to worry about repairs or depreciation. You just pay your monthly bills, and at the end of the lease period, you go get a new car. Since I've been out of school, that's worked the best for me.

—CHRISTOPHER
HAVERTOWN, PENNSYLVANIA

. . . .

"Unless you're really rich, always buy used cars. It's just a smart financial decision because cars lose so much of their value in the first year anyway."

—ROBERT SALTER
MÖNCHENGLADBACK, GERMANY

. . . .

SET A BUDGET AND STICK TO IT. My husband and I budget every month. We put our money into three categories. Fifty percent goes to necessities, 25 percent goes to wants, and 25 percent goes to savings. If we exceed the amount set aside for necessities, then it comes out of wants. The whole goal is to save that 25 percent. It has worked really well. I save every receipt. If we exceed our budget for the month, the next month, we go without.

—ANONYMOUS
KIRKSVILLE, MISSOURI

BUY A CAR, OR ELSE!

My father always said that you have to shop around for the best price in everything, including cars. He also said you can't be afraid to walk out of a dealership. I decided to follow this advice when I went out to buy my first car. I made a list of the Ford dealers in the area and started visiting them all. I knew that no one would get my business that day. No matter what, I would take their best offer home for consideration.

My plan was working fine when I walked into the last place on my list. It was the one closest to home. I was talking about models and pricing with the salesman when he casually asked me for my keys. He said my old car was blocking some other cars that needed to be moved. I didn't think anything of it.

When we were done I said thanks, shook his hand, and told him I'd be in touch. When I got out to my car, I realized I hadn't gotten my keys back. I went back in and told the salesman, but he refused to give them back. He said that we had to complete our deal first. I laughed and politely asked again. He said no. I was furious. I demanded my keys, but he sat there like a statue. I'm guessing he had some luck with this tactic before, probably with young people like me. I walked out the door, found a pay phone, and called the police. The cop who answered the phone laughed when I told him what was going on but said he'd send someone right over.

It didn't occur to me until right before my dad walked into the showroom that he was on duty that day and that he might very well be the cop who would be sent. He just looked at me and laughed. The salesman was out of his seat and across the floor in an instant with the keys in his hand. My dad never said a word to him. He just stared at him and took the keys. That night Dad asked me if I wanted him to come with me the next time I went car shopping. I said only if he agreed to wear his uniform.

—RAEANN BLACK
LEETONIA, OHIO

WHEN BUYING A CAR, you've got to be willing to walk away, because sometimes that's the only way to get what you want. The dealership was trying to charge me an extra $150 handling fee, and I said forget it and turned to leave. Suddenly, the guy started chasing me down. Guess what? They waived the fee.

—*RANDY FREITIK*
PEORIA, ILLINOIS

• • • • • • • •

UNDERSTAND THAT ISSUES like banking and insurance are not black and white. Those organizations have some wiggle room in terms of who they do business with and what kinds of rates are given. With that in mind, it's important to go meet these people in person when signing up to use their services. Don't do it over the phone. When I did that, I made sure that I looked my best. I figured if I walked into the bank where I would be doing my banking for the next several years wearing leather pants, I would not get the same service as if I walked in wearing a nice business suit, which is what I did. First impressions are important. And with car insurance people, keep in mind that as a young adult you are a high risk to them to begin with. So you want to look as mature as possible when you meet them, to alleviate some of those fears.

—*PAM WAXTER*
KEEZLETOWN, VIRGINIA

• • • • • • • •

I DON'T THINK I'VE EVER BOUGHT CLOTHES if they weren't on sale, and I rarely use my credit card. I made a conscious decision not to have credit card debt in my life, so I will only purchase something if I know I can pay for it.

—*MARIANA*
SAN FRANCISCO, CALIFORNIA

I WENT THROUGH A PHASE of saving like crazy. I felt this strange panic if I didn't have enough money in my savings account to leave the country and go somewhere amazing at the drop of a hat. This is a hard time in your life to deny yourself instant gratification. But man, it can pay off in the long run.

—*F.S.*
CHAPEL HILL, NORTH CAROLINA

If you have to borrow to buy it, then you can't afford it!

—*SHANNON*
LAS VEGAS,
NEVADA

• • • • • • • • •

CREDIT CARD COMPANIES CAN BE DECEIVING. It's kind of like being stranded at sea. Just when you're about to max out one credit card and miss out on that trip to Vegas, along comes another credit card company to throw you what appears to be a life vest in the form of an application for another credit card. It's not until you apply for your first car loan or home mortgage years later that you realize what they threw you was not a life vest, but an anvil. How do you stay afloat? Tread water. Stop living beyond your means.

—*KENNETH C. RINEY*
DALLAS, TEXAS

• • • • • • • • •

ONCE YOU START WORKING AND GETTING a regular paycheck, you have to do at least two things with the money. First, set a certain amount that you will put in a savings account no matter what. Second, set an amount that will be your mad money—money you can spend any way you want without feeling guilty. I did both of those things and found that the key is sticking to the set amounts, no matter what. If your mad money for the week is gone and your friends want to go out, then you have to show some self-control and stay in.

—*SHERRI LAWTON*
HARRISONBURG, VIRGINIA

IF YOU'RE EVER IN THE POSITION to buy a house and a car at the same time, pick the house first because it's a much better investment.

—*SHANNON HURD*
HIGHLANDS RANCH, COLORADO

• • • • • • • •

YOU SHOULD ALWAYS KEEP ENOUGH money in your savings account to last you at least a month. You never know when you will find yourself out of work. I ended up quitting my first job after about a year when my boss asked me to do something that I thought was unethical. I was unsure for a while if I was going to be able to collect unemployment or not. Luckily I had a nest egg tucked away to sustain me. Otherwise I would have had to move back in with my parents.

—*BILL STUDENA*
FLORENCE, KENTUCKY

• • • • • • • •

IT PAYS TO PAY OFF DEBT, especially when you make just enough to get by. What is starting to help me pay it down is switching credit card companies. Look in the mail for credit card offers that give you zero percent interest for 12 to 16 months. I asked a financial adviser about this, and he said that as long as you have an OK credit score, this won't hurt you to do every year or so. Just keep shopping for the zero percent interest until you can pay it off.

—*JERALYN*
AUSTIN, TEXAS

• • • • • • • •

SMART COUPLES FINISH RICH by David Bach is the best money book I've ever read. It walks you step by step through every part of the financial planning process, and it doesn't use fancy terms.

—*S.A.*
LAKE FOREST, CALIFORNIA

YOU, THE CONSUMER

In the 12 months following graduation, two out of every five graduates will buy a car; half will establish new wireless phone service.

BUDGETING IS ROUGH, BUT BE PATIENT. I only eat out once or twice a week, and I make cheap things at home, like mac and cheese, the other days. And I furnish my apartment slowly. It still isn't all finished, but I haven't had to feel completely broke, either.

—*CHERYL*
PHILADELPHIA, PENNSYLVANIA

• • • • • • • •

"Set aside time to do your finances every week. Go to a café. Order your favorite drink. Take 45 minutes to make sure you've got everything in order. You will sleep better at night and have more fun when you go out."

—*J.A.*
ATLANTA, GEORGIA

• • • • • • • •

USE CREDIT CARDS AS EMERGENCY ONLY, and stick to that. Don't shop for everyday items with them; it only gets you into more debt and more trouble. Your credit rating is *very* important, even when it doesn't seem so important when you're young. It can haunt you for a long time after you screw up!

—*BECKIE*
SEATTLE, WASHINGTON

INSTEAD OF GOING ON A TRIP, I took the money I received for graduation and paid off my credit card. They warned us in college about the pitfalls of credit-card debt. I decided that I didn't want to start out with that hanging over my head. I had one credit card, and I cut it up after I paid it off. That was a good day.

—*SUZI MACK*
BENTON, MISSOURI

• • • • • • • •

TALK WITH SOMEONE ABOUT your personal finances. My first year out of college, I had no idea what to do about my taxes. I was lucky, though, because my uncle was able to guide me. For instance, I signed up to make a weekly contribution to United Way through my employer. My contribution is tax deductible. There are computer programs to help you prepare your taxes, but I would recommend you consult someone you trust the first time you do your taxes.

—*JULIE MCKITRICK*
ST. LOUIS, MISSOURI

• • • • • • • •

WHEN THE STATE SAYS they want their student loan money paid back by a certain time, they mean it. Don't figure that you'll be able to skate around that or extend that loan forever. They will get serious on you. I had a hard time finding a good job after college, so I had a hard time paying the loan back. They gave me an extension, but when I fell behind again, they took my entire tax return check one year to get their money. It still wasn't enough. I made payments to pay it off. Those guys play hardball.

—*JASON HAMES*
DRY RIDGE, KENTUCKY

NO MATTER HOW POOR YOU ARE, you'd better have enough money to buy your mother a birthday present. The first year I lived alone, I was plumb broke and didn't even get her a card. I stupidly thought she'd understand because she knew I was struggling to find work. But she was really hurt by that. I guess I could have borrowed the money. The next year I was working, and I went all out for her birthday. I even had a special cake made for her. But I never forgot the look in her eyes when I showed up empty-handed that first year. Find a way to show Mom how much she means, no matter what.

—*TIMOTHY QUIGLEY*
INDEPENDENCE, KENTUCKY

• • • • • • • • •

I DON'T LIKE SHOPPING and I don't bother going out for food if my fridge is empty. I guess that's why I often wake up hungry. I have nothing on my walls and live a very basic existence. It works for me!

—*BRIAN*
NEW YORK, NEW YORK

• • • • • • • • •

MY HUSBAND WENT CRAZY with credit cards (before we met, of course) and racked up over $10,000 worth of charges. Three years later he had nothing to show for it—the TV was broken, the tires needed to be replaced, the car stereo died—and he realized what a mistake he made. Six years later we are still waiting for those charges to fall off his credit. Together we decided to only use credit in case of an emergency. Credit is really a loan, not free money, and if you want it badly enough, save up for it and pay cash!

—*VANESSA*
HOUSTON, TEXAS

It stinks not being able to go out and buy everything I want, but I am determined to stick to a budget. My weakness is eating out. Now, I make myself go home and find something in the refrigerator to eat. I save up for special occasions to eat out with friends. It's paying off, because I'm finally starting to build my savings account.

> —TAWNY WHITE
> SPRINGFIELD, MISSOURI

College was one of the best times of my life, thanks to Mr. MasterCard and Mrs. Visa!

> —JERALYN
> AUSTIN, TEXAS

Start contributing to your 401(k). I wish I had done that sooner. I know I still have plenty of time before retirement, but I kept thinking it would lower my paycheck. Then I sat down and did the math. I realized that since the money comes out before taxes, my check was actually only $2 less each time. That's a very small sacrifice to make to know I'm building something for my future. Basically, I see a 401(k) as sort of free money, where your employer is willing to match it. It's one of the best and easiest things to take advantage of.

> —RANDALL S. WRAY
> MUNCIE, INDIANA

Buy a house as soon as you can. It sounds crazy, I know, but it isn't. If you can pay rent, you can buy a house. Do it before you go and mess up your credit. Find out about first-time homeowner's loans, and find out if you have access to grant money, especially if you work for the state. I got a job with the state for that very reason. Don't worry if it's not the house of your dreams. In five or ten years you can move out and rent it for the same as your mortgage payments, or sell it and go bigger.

> —CHRIS
> CHAPEL HILL, NORTH CAROLINA

I'VE GIVEN UP ONE OF MY FAVORITE HOBBIES, shopping, because I live in New York and have to try to save. Now, if I want to go shopping, I decide to get one thing instead of a million.

—MARA
NEW YORK, NEW YORK

• • • • • • • •

REMEMBER THE ACRONYM EMILY: Early Money Is Like Yeast. It grows and grows. The money you put away in your twenties will be a huge pot of gold for your future. For many people, an automatic savings plan that deducts from their paycheck is the least painful option. Think of it as one CD and two grande cappucinos a week. You can do it!

—N.
BROOKLYN, NEW YORK

• • • • • • • •

DON'T EXPECT TO GET THE BEST APARTMENT and car out of school. Once you're in debt, it's so hard to climb out. If you stay out of debt, you can work your way into something great.

—BRODIE
SITKA, ALASKA

• • • • • • • •

A LOT OF FINANCIAL BOOKS WILL TELL YOU that you need six months' worth of salary in the bank as a cushion in case you lose your job. Who can have that kind of money in the bank when they're just out of college? As a recent grad, you need to just concentrate on paying off any debt. If there's anything left over after your bills, put that in savings. But don't kick yourself if you're not financially stable by the time you're 25.

—MICHELE
HOLLY, MICHIGAN

The Inner You: On Health & Spirituality

A simple truth: *There is a finite amount of beer and midnight pizza dinners one body can take before the effects start to show. In other words, part of the fun in college is enjoying relatively good health without even thinking about it. But sooner or later (it's getting sooner by the minute), you will have to work to stay healthy. We talked with other recent grads about how they've learned to juggle a new life with healthy habits and the spiritual changes they undergo as they set out on their own. Read on to find out how to stay happy with yourself, inside and out.*

QUIT SMOKING *NOW*. You won't do it later. This is true for cigarettes and marijuana. They can be youthful indiscretions only so long as you're young. After that, they will control your budget and your social life in ways you don't realize.

—ERIKA
TALLAHASSEE, FLORIDA

REMEMBER: KETCHUP AND MUSTARD ARE NOT VEGETABLES.

—J.D.
UNITY, OHIO

HEAD LINES
Best Advice and Top Tips

- Eat right and exercise in your 20s; the habit will go a long way later in life.

- If you are lucky enough to have health insurance, use it.

- Make a list of things that make you happy and post it where you can see it every day.

- Don't give up your spirituality in pursuit of your career.

- Try to maintain a sense of balance within your body and your mind.

Know that spirituality is different from religion.

—BRANDI
DICOSTANZO
DALLAS, TEXAS

PUT SPIRITUALITY FIRST. When I graduated college, I immediately jumped into pursuing my career. I was very materialistic; my main goal in life was to own a BMW by age 30. I jumped from job to job, working first for an author, then becoming a newspaper reporter, then starting my own business as a fitness trainer. Unfortunately, while I was good at everything I tried, I had a lot of trouble finding inner satisfaction with anything. It wasn't until I went on a yoga retreat five years ago and met my spiritual teacher that my life started to change for the better. I now realize that unless you have spiritual satisfaction in your life, no amount of professional success will ever satisfy you.

—ROBIN
HARTFORD, CONNECTICUT

WHILE I WAS IN COLLEGE, my mom told me I should start taking multivitamins. I did it just to shut her up, but I was surprised how much better they made me feel. It didn't happen overnight, but over a period of months I realized that I had more energy than before, and that I seemed to get sick less than before, and my thinking even seemed clearer.

—*JASMINE MATRE*
COVINGTON, KENTUCKY

" I try to avoid discussions with my mom about what I'm going to do with my life. She just freaks me out even more. "

—*MARA*
NEW YORK, NEW YORK

SPIRITUAL PRINCIPLES ARE IMPORTANT, but you can't use them as an excuse to ignore basic human incompatibilities. I'm a very spiritual person. A while back, I was feeling a lot of insecurity, fear, and anxiety in my relationship. I brushed aside these feelings and told myself, "Everything will be OK if only I can learn to forgive," or "God will work everything out in the long run." Basically, I was using the spiritual principles I believed in so firmly to deny what I was feeling on an emotional level. By the time I realized what I was doing, the relationship, along with my peace of mind, had deteriorated.

—*SAJIT GREENE*
UTICA, NEW YORK

THE KEY IS BALANCE. I still splurge and enjoy a big bowl of ice cream every now and then. I just make sure that I also exercise a bit more that day. It's unrealistic to try to banish something that you like from your life.

—*JENNIFER*
KANSAS CITY, MISSOURI

Most of the spiritual experiences I had before I was 30 were drug-induced.

—*PETER STEUR*
BRISBANE,
AUSTRALIA

I'VE STARTED TAKING CLASSES AT THE Y—kickboxing, step aerobics, interval training, and sculpting. It gives you a reason to force yourself to work out. Also, it's a great way to meet fun people. I find myself looking forward to going back just to see how they're doing.

—*JAYME BOGGIANO*
ST. LOUIS, MISSOURI

STAYING HEALTHY IN YOUR 20S is probably the hardest thing ever. You have just graduated from every chance to really play on a supercompetitive sports team, and you find yourself working all through the day just to crawl home with a desire to go get cocktails. The easiest way to stay healthy would be to join a gym nearby. Also, get into sushi.

—*JENNI BACKES*
SEATTLE, WASHINGTON

MAKE DEALS WITH YOURSELF. I'd promise myself that if I could sit through an hour-long mass on Sundays, I'd allow myself to go out to the bar on Tuesdays. And the beauty of it was that my parents didn't have to know about the deal. All they knew was that I went to mass on Sunday. It's a good way to start acting like an adult but give yourself a little reward, too.

—*MIKE POUND*
UNITY, OHIO

I HAVE GOTTEN IN THE HABIT OF GETTING out of bed before work, throwing on my running clothes, and doing three quick miles. Then I come home, put on the coffee, take a hot shower, and have a nice breakfast. I've found that getting the day off to a good, healthy start like that is invaluable. It just gets the day pointed in the right direction, and it creates positive momentum that can last through the whole day.

—*JALLE LITTLE*
INDEPENDENCE, KENTUCKY

* * * * * * * *

" Just because the girl you brought home from the club later says, 'Oh God,' in the bedroom, that does not constitute having gone to church. Not by a long shot. "

—*TED VALKO*
CHURCHILL, OHIO

* * * * * * * *

FAITH IS A HARD SELL to most 23-year-olds if they don't already have it, and most, even if they grew up in a church, don't have real faith. I went through a long period where I relied on Eastern practices to fill that gap for me—meditation and yoga. It helped. I was able to pay attention to the spiritual without compromising my sense of curiosity. I advocate experimentation at that time of life, exploring different faiths.

—*F.S.*
CHAPEL HILL, NORTH CAROLINA

Go to church.
It won't kill
you.

—*FLORA JANICKI*
FLORENCE,
KENTUCKY

ALL A MATTER OF PERSPECTIVE

PRETEND THIS IS A TV SHOW. No matter what happens, imagine reading in *TV Guide* that this is the plot for our show this week. Like, "Joey misses the bus leaving Chattanooga, and he's stranded there until someone notices." That really happened— the bus took off without me. I just sat on the bus bench until it came back. It took about an hour. The point is, it could be any- thing, or it could be nothing, but everyone  can have his own TV show. It helps you cope with problems bet- ter, because nothing seems as serious.

　　—JOEY
　　　CAPE COD, MASSACHUSETTS

● ● ● ● ● ● ● ●

WHENEVER I HAVE A PROBLEM, and it seems really big, and it's really stressing me out, it helps me to look down on it from far away. The phrase in my head is, "Look at it from space." This helps me get along with difficult people in any area, because I think, "This really isn't such a big deal in the grand scheme of things." Instead of looking at a person's angry red face, I look at it from another planet, because it takes all of the personal stuff out of it. It separates you emotionally from what is going on.

　　—KAMI
　　　CAPE COD, MASSACHUSETTS

I ENDED UP HAVING A BREAKDOWN in college and going to a hospital for it. The one thing I learned is that it's important to lean on other people. Don't isolate yourself. I was very fortunate to have a lot of people in my life that cared about me. Breakdowns are more common than you think. In my case, it turned out that I was diagnosed bipolar, which is pretty serious. I had to see someone about that and take regular medication. A lot of good things came from that. I'm realizing I'm mortal, there are limits to what I can do, and I need to be sensitive to those limits.

—*ANONYMOUS*
LOS ANGELES, CALIFORNIA

• • • • • • • •

MAKE A LIST OF FIVE TO TEN SMALL THINGS that put a smile on your face and post it where you can see it every day. I used to have a very destructive habit: When I got stressed out, I stopped doing things I knew would make me feel better, like calling a friend, going for a walk, or taking a hot bath. Instead, I'd do negative things, like overeat, lie on the couch, and channel surf, because I was stuck in a downhill spiral of bad feelings. Fortunately, it was an easy habit to break. I made a list of fun things to do. It was an effective reminder that doing even one small thing can send you in a positive direction.

—*SAJIT GREENE*
UTICA, NEW YORK

• • • • • • • •

START EVERY MORNING WITH A BLOODY MARY. You can tell people that it has tomato juice and celery. There's nothing wrong with those things. You can leave out the part about the vodka if it makes you feel uncomfortable.

—*J.G.*
JAMESTOWN, NEW YORK

✔

Am I more spiritual as an adult? No. I never was spiritual, and I don't think I ever will be. Smarter? Yes. Wiser? Yes.

—*CHERI RIOT*
MISSION VIEJO
CALIFORNIA

EVEN IF YOU'RE NOT RELIGIOUS, a rear pew in a beautiful church is a great place to just think things over.

—*N.*
BROOKLYN, NEW YORK

• • • • • • • •

66 Don't overestimate the power and allure of the elements. Why has mankind enjoyed the sight of the sunset or sunrise for thousands of years? Because it's cool and elemental. It connects you to your core self. 99

—*MICHAEL*
SAN FRANCISCO, CALIFORNIA

• • • • • • • •

AT LEAST ONCE A YEAR, I go to a different religious service at a different house of worship. It can be a variation of Christianity, Buddhism, Judaism, Muslim, whatever. The important thing is that it shows me how other people get in tune with their version of God, and it feels good to do it. For those who are seeking something different from how they were raised, I highly recommend this. One day out of the year is not much, but it's really rewarding.

—*J.A.*
ATLANTA, GEORGIA

I ALWAYS SAY THAT I HAVE GOD IN MY HEART, and that is where I celebrate him. Spirituality is what you make of it. I don't believe in going to church or going through the rituals required by certain religions. In my heart I know what is true, and it is there that my spirituality is prosperous.

—*HEATHER POLLOCK*
ORANGE COUNTY, CALIFORNIA

• • • • • • • •

PRACTICE CONSISTENCY. Life isn't so much about making huge leaps every once in a while as it is taking small steps every day. Right now, for example, I'm trying to market myself as a personal coach. Instead of not calling anybody for a month, and then suddenly making 150 phone calls in one day, I make a point to talk to five people each day about my new business. This approach is much less stressful and, in the end, puts me in a better position to come out on top.

—*ROBIN*
HARTFORD, CONNECTICUT

• • • • • • • •

MY FAMILY DIDN'T GO TO CHURCH when I was growing up. About a year after I graduated from college, I realized that something was missing in my life. I decided that I wanted to join a church. My boyfriend and I began visiting churches in the area. A number of churches offer classes that you can attend to learn about the principles of the religion. I think it's really important to know about the church and understand the doctrine. We eventually found a church that was a good fit for us. I can't explain what it was that drew us to this particular church. It felt really comfortable.

—*LISA*
NIXA, MISSOURI

I play golf and do yoga. It helps alleviate stress and keeps me more focused at work.

—*GEHONG WANG*
ROCKVILLE
MARYLAND

TO INSURE, OR NOT TO INSURE

HEALTH INSURANCE IS A LARGE PART OF WHY I avoid the doctor. I've found that health insurance companies truly exist to not help you. I've been more or less cheated by nearly every health insurance company I've been affiliated with.

—*I.B.*
INDIANAPOLIS, INDIANA

• • • • • • • •

DON'T BEAT YOURSELF UP ABOUT not having health insurance. If I could afford it, I would, but I'm a musician. I'm not going to give up what I love for a job with benefits. Instead, I eat really well. I'm a vegetarian, I eat organic produce, I work out, and I laugh a lot. I think that helps a person not get sick.

—*KAMI*
CAPE COD, MASSACHUSETTS

• • • • • • • •

GET HEALTH INSURANCE. It's worth the cost for the peace of mind. There was a time for about six months when I didn't have any. I remember that I was in a dance concert, and I was scared to death that I was going to break something. It was a scary time.

—*MEGHAN*
MASCOUTAH, ILLINOIS

IF YOU HAVE ACCEPTED A JOB that has health, dental, and vision insurance, use it. There is a reason it is called a "benefit." I look at it as money that is available for me to use if I choose to use it. I get $125 every two years to put toward contacts or glasses; I'm an idiot if I don't take advantage of that. Also, don't get off a schedule of going to the doctor or dentist, because much like a gym, it becomes easier never to go back. I skipped two years of visits to the dentist, and it is going to cost me more in the end, with more drastic procedures and pain.

—JAMES RINEY
FORT WORTH, TEXAS

• • • • • • • • •

IF YOU DON'T HAVE HEALTH INSURANCE, you can take college classes and qualify for the group insurance rates, which are much cheaper. Insurance for my family was going to be $800 a month. Once I signed up for classes, however, I got six months for $2,000.

—RANDY FREITIK
PEORIA, ILLINOIS

HMO VS. PPO

Consumer Reports surveyed more than 35,000 readers about their HMOs and PPOs. The best-reviewed plans are featured at www.consumerreports.org.

EXPERIMENT WITH HEALTHY FOODS. When you were living at home, you probably got the same fruits and vegetables from your mother. Moms tend to stick with what works. But don't be afraid to experiment. When I moved out on my own, I went to the produce section of the market and bought all kinds of things that I had never tried before. I didn't even know what most of them were, but I figured if they were produce, they had to be good for me. I found a real love for kiwi, which I had never been exposed to at home.

—COLIN MCDOUGLE
CANFIELD, OHIO

• • • • • • • •

IT'S HARD TO KEEP A HEALTHY LIFESTYLE in a big city because there are a ton of bad influences: poor air quality, smokers, drinkers, etc. But I walk a lot, work out at the gym, take vitamins, and don't drink or smoke in order to maintain a healthy lifestyle.

—ANONYMOUS
NEW YORK, NEW YORK

• • • • • • • •

IF YOU DECIDE TO STAY with your parents' religion, understand that this will make them very, very happy. So don't spoil it by letting them find out that you are not going to church every Sunday. You should go, but if you don't go, just keep it a secret. A little white lie like that won't upset God too much. He'll forgive you for the peace of mind that you are giving your mom.

—TOM BURDOCK
POLAND, OHIO

BE TRUE TO YOURSELF. I was raised Roman Catholic by two very religious parents. I went to church and Sunday school every single week as a child. As I grew older, I started to realize that there were a lot of things that the church teaches that I didn't really believe. I didn't know how to deal with it, so I just kept on keeping on. I didn't want to rock the boat. But once I got out on my own and started going to church alone on Sundays, it started to seem silly. Here I was spending all this time in a church that was teaching ideas that I didn't agree with. I was afraid to stop going because I knew it would kill my mother. One day I stopped at my parents' house and had a long talk with my mom about religion. To my surprise, she was cool about it. She said I had to follow my heart and that she wouldn't want me to spend the rest of my life living a lie.

> —STAN SHENK
> HARRISONBURG, VIRGINIA

• • • • • • • •

GROWING UP, WE HAD SHABBAT (Sabbath) dinner every Friday night and celebrated all the holidays in wonderful ways. I now know that traditions are really important and I also realize the extent of the effort that must go in. It's worth it to do these things. Being single in the big city—and not having my family here—I feel a bit uprooted. I don't have an automatic religious context. I notice it. I want to start a Friday night dinner club with my friends, but we still haven't because it takes time.

> —JANNA
> VANCOUVER, BRITISH COLUMBIA, CANADA

Eat well and go outside. That works for me.

—LOUIS HAGMAN
SEATTLE
WASHINGTON

THE KEY TO STAYING HEALTHY is to build sports and activity into your life. I really miss working out when I am not able to. Essentially, I have replaced the hard-ass coach I had in high school with a little voice in my head reminding me to work out, to set goals, and to feel good about myself when I succeed.

—*STEPHEN MACKAY*
SOUTH ORANGE, NEW JERSEY

• • • • • • • •

THERE ARE MANY WAYS I maintain a healthy lifestyle in New York. I used to belong to a gym, I have taken yoga, and now I take dance classes. I also use the outdoors as my playground. If you are near Central Park, like me, you can enjoy a variety of outdoor activities there (weather permitting, of course).

—*LISA GREENBAUM*
NEW YORK, NEW YORK

• • • • • • • •

WORKING OUT AND EATING HEALTHY on a regular basis (i.e., not eating candy and Pop-Tarts for breakfast, lunch and dinner) will keep you feeling good. Also, practice good dental hygiene. It's expensive and painful not to care about your teeth!

—*TAI DAVIS*
PALATINE, ILLINOIS

• • • • • • • •

I PLAY SOCCER, TENNIS, AND BASKETBALL and get recharged for work this way. In these games, we're allowed to yell at each other, and this helps me release tension from the real world!

—*CENIK*
KAZAKHSTAN

More Wisdom: Good Stuff That Doesn't Fit Anywhere Else

When you were living at home and having Mom act as your personal maid and Dad handle money-management duties (or vice versa), you probably heard your parents say one too many times, "After you graduate college and enter the real world, you're going to be in for a rude awakening." It's true. But short of stopping the hands of time or lining yourself up with a spot in a nice psychiatric ward, it's impossible to avoid it. Which is why we've gathered "life advice" from our respondents. Here's wishing you good luck, and welcome to your life.

IF YOU FIND YOURSELF counting among your accomplishments your high score on "Doom," you are not yet living in the real world, and perhaps you should take a break from your computer. There's a whole life out there waiting for you.

—J.A.
ATLANTA, GEORGIA

GET RID OF CABLE! READ A BOOK INSTEAD.

—SHANNON
LAS VEGAS, NEVADA

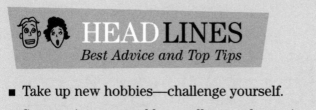

HEAD LINES
Best Advice and Top Tips

- Take up new hobbies—challenge yourself.

- Success is measured by small, everyday actions, not by the size of your bank account.

- Write a letter to yourself outlining your hopes and dreams and put it away for the future.

- Don't let the day-to-day pressure make you forget what a gift life is.

- Hope for everything, but expect nothing—that way you will be pleasantly surprised.

Never skimp on Q-tips and toilet paper.

*—Jennifer
Seattle,
Washington*

ALWAYS KEEP A PAIR OF COMFORTABLE old shoes in the trunk of your car. You never know when you are going to break down and will need to walk to get help. Don't think just because you have a cell phone that you'll be able to call for help. It may not work or you may not be able to get a connection. One time I was driving home from a wedding by myself late at night. I was on a rural road in the middle of nowhere and got a flat tire. My phone wouldn't work, and I had to walk to a gas station. The only shoes I had were the uncomfortable dress shoes I had on. By the time I found help, I had blisters on my toes. After that, I always keep old tennis shoes in the trunk.

*—John Fairfield
Harrisonburg, Virginia*

SUCCESS ISN'T MEASURED by HEMIs or McMansions, bank accounts or bling. Success is measured in the subtlety of life and in your everyday decisions. I'd sing praises to hear that you kept a tree from being cut down or a faucet from dripping. I'd be saddened to hear you live alone in an 8,000-square-foot home 30 miles from work. Keep it simple. And, oh yeah, girls don't like the smell of patchouli.

—*ED AKINS II*
STATESBORO, GEORGIA

· · · · · · · ·

" Learn how to spell the word *weird*. I can't tell you how many really smart people write *wierd*. "

—*ANDREA*
TORONTO, ONTARIO, CANADA

· · · · · · · ·

I RECENTLY TOOK UP PIANO, though I'm not musically inclined by nature. I did this to challenge myself and get out of my comfort zone. When you take up new hobbies that you've never tried and may not even be naturally good at, it helps keep other areas of your life fresh. You're challenging your brain to think in a new way, and when you go back to the real world things feel newer and more exciting.

—*JEFF MALTZ*
SAN FRANCISCO, CALIFORNIA

YOU CAN DO IT!

Have patience with yourself. I moved hours from home after college. When I had to go back to my apartment, all I could do was sit on my couch, littered with unpacked bins, and cry. Part of me wanted to just call up the newspaper and say, "Yeah, you know when I accepted this job? I was just kidding." But luckily, I have a good friend who gives me "tough love." She basically explained to me that it's supposed to suck at first when you leave everything you're used to, and that I needed to give it three months.

Well, it's been three months. Not an easy three months, but I've made it, and I'm staying. It's a strange feeling to be so in charge of your own life. I've never been so accountable for my actions. You stop thinking of yourself as just a part of your family and think about what it will be like to start your own branch of the family tree.

There will be good days and bad days. Sometimes you'll be so happy with your decision to start your career, but there will also be the days where you would give anything to rewind your life and go back to your college days. But instead of thinking you already lived the best years of your life, I prefer to think that you have some good years left in you.

—CHERYL
PHILADELPHIA, PENNSYLVANIA

CLEANLINESS IS KEY. To avoid messiness, I clean in quick spurts, often. I don't want to put a Sunday aside for cleaning my place, so I Swiffer the floors while I brush my teeth in the morning. I actually like keeping my place in shape.

—*BRIAN*
NEW YORK, NEW YORK

WHEN YOU CHANGE ADDRESSES (no matter how many times), always immediately do a change of address through the USPS. It is annoying for the next tenant to have to forward mail of yours that looks urgent, and to deal with your abandoned copies of *International Male*.

—*T.M.*
ATLANTA, GEORGIA

Hope for everything and expect nothing. That way, when something good happens you appreciate it, and when something bad happens it doesn't get you down.

—*H.O.*
EVERETT
WASHINGTON

I THINK THE GREATEST CHALLENGE of living in the "real world"—of living, period—is finding ways to nurture your own sense of freedom and happiness in life, to keep all the pressures from making life feel more like a chore or a burden than the strange gift it really is.

—*JOE*
BOSTON, MASSACHUSETTS

WATCH THE NEWS MORE and have your own point of view. It's important to do these things as an adult. Be more educated. The news is a good place to start, and you may find connections with people that way.

—*MICHAEL ALBERT PAOLI*
TORONTO, ONTARIO, CANADA

WRITE YOURSELF A LETTER OF ADVICE NOW, talking about your hopes and worries about the future. Put that letter away in a sock drawer or at the back of your filing cabinet. When you find it, read it.

—*J.P.*
CHARLOTTESVILLE, VIRGINIA

• • • • • • • •

I THINK WE COME OUT OF SCHOOL with this idea of what we want to do, primarily based on what we want to wear while we are doing it. I wanted to be a high-powered PR girl in a high-rise building with a corner office. I would wear a gray Gucci skirt suit with beautiful Michael Kors shoes. I would tell people to do what I wanted and I'd be really skinny, with a great complexion. Never mind the work!

—*STASIA RAINES*
SAN DIEGO, CALIFORNIA

• • • • • • • •

APPRECIATE THE THINGS THAT OTHERS DO for you. My boyfriend and best friend really helped me with my first week of work; taking care of my dog and fixing breakfast. Having people you can depend on to help you through transitions, even if it's a friend across the country whom you can call, is one of the most fulfilling ways to success. Just make sure you return the favor when they need it!

—*LACEY CONNELLY*
CHICAGO, ILLINOIS

• • • • • • • •

LEARN HOW TO BE A GOOD SALESPERSON, without dressing and acting like a salesperson.

—*ZACH MARTEN*
DALLAS, TEXAS

I **ALWAYS STICK TO THE SAYING,** "Doubt means don't." I have become less impulsive in my decision-making. Once you are in the real world you are solely responsible for your decisions.

—*CASEY BOND*
GRAND RAPIDS, MICHIGAN

• • • • • • • •

JUST REALIZE THAT AS HARD AS THINGS SEEM at first, they'll get better. I've learned that lots of things won't make sense until you look back at them down the road.

—*ANONYMOUS*
NEW YORK, NEW YORK

• • • • • • • •

TO **LIVE THE LIFE YOU WANT,** you have to 1) know what you want, and 2) go after what you want. You have to live intentionally, not accidentally. It took me a long time to figure that out.

—*N.*
BROOKLYN, NEW YORK

• • • • • • • •

YOU **NEED TWO THINGS TO STAY IN SHAPE:** Someone to work out with, and a sports league or regular pickup league to join. I work out three times a week, but I probably wouldn't do it if I knew my buddy wasn't going to be there, waiting on me. And vice versa. Also, I play basketball on Wednesday nights in a YMCA league. I look forward to it during the week, and it keeps me active and in shape.

—*ALAN*
MEMPHIS, TENNESSEE

ALWAYS BE BUSY. Sitting around and not being busy is really dangerous. It gets you in a funk. Even you're doing something lame, do something to keep you busy.

—BRODIE
SITKA, ALASKA

• • • • • • • •

SPIRITUALITY IS DIFFERENT FOR EVERYONE. I like to read *A River Runs Through It* and go fly-fishing. That's all I need.

—ALAN
MEMPHIS, TENNESSEE

REAL WORLD
INFORMATION

OPENING YOUR OWN BANK ACCOUNT

These days, you can easily open a checking or savings account by walking into any bank with proof of address, age, and personal identification. You can also sign up over the phone or through online banking sites. But you want to make sure you're signing up for a bank that's right for you. Here are a few standard questions to consider when you open an account:

- ❏ What is the monthly fee for the account, if any?

- ❏ Is the account FDIC-insured? (Make sure they answer "yes" to this; it means you'll get your money back if the bank goes bankrupt.)

- ❏ What is the fee for using an ATM machine that belongs to another bank?

- ❏ Is there a minimum balance that I must keep? And what sorts of fees apply if I go below the limit?

- ❏ Is there a limit to the amount of transactions I may make in a month? What sorts of fees apply if I go over that limit?

- ❏ What is the interest rate of my savings account? Are there charges if I go below the minimum balance?

BUYING A USED CAR

It's common knowledge that as soon as you drive a new car off the lot, you lose 15 to 30 percent of what you paid for it. As someone who is just getting started in your financial life, this is a good enough reason to buy something used. You'll pay less, get a better "drive off the lot" deal, and feel better about yourself.

That said, watch out for car salesmen trying to unload a junker. Here are some tips to follow so that you'll wind up with the best car for your money.

❑ Once you find a car you like, have an independent mechanic inspect it. This usually costs around $100, and it could save you thousands in future repairs if he spots something wrong with the car.

❑ Have the dealer show you the car's inspection history. If they won't show it to you—or say they don't have it—consider that a red flag.

❑ Write down the car's Vehicle Identification Number, or VIN, and run it through a national database such as CARFAX. You'll get the car's full history, including odometer readings, accidents, and sales.

❑ Read the warranty and make sure you understand what is covered and what is not.

❑ Bottom line: never buy a car without sleeping on the final offer first. No matter what a salesman tells you, you can always come back tomorrow.

YOUR FIST KITCHEN

Whether you hate to cook, love to cook, or are somewhere in between, you do need to eat. If you eat take-out food all the time you'll go broke. If you eat ramen noodles all the time, you'll die of malnutrition. You'll just have to use that kitchen.

It doesn't have to be your parents' well-equipped, haute-cuisine establishment. The fact is, you don't need a lot of fancy (expensive) equipment to turn out delicious, nutritious meals. Here's a list of the basics you'll need in order to cook for yourself.

TIP: You can find many of these items at tag sales and Salvation Army stores. Cast iron is easily refurbished, takes light maintenance, but lasts forever and is well worth it.

EQUIPMENT

- ❑ 1.5 or 2-quart saucepan
- ❑ 6-quart saucepan
- ❑ 10- or 12-quart soup or stock pot, each with a lid to fit
- ❑ 1 10"cast-iron skillet
- ❑ 1 6" cast-iron skillet
- ❑ A 6" chef's knife
- ❑ A paring knife
- ❑ A cleaver
- ❑ A few long-handled wooden spoons
- ❑ 1 long-handled slotted spoon
- ❑ 1 long-handled ladle (8 oz.)
- ❑ 1 spatula
- ❑ 1-quart Pyrex measuring cup
- ❑ 1 set of dry measuring cups
- ❑ 1 set of measuring spoons
- ❑ 1 colander
- ❑ 1 mesh strainer
- ❑ 1 can opener/bottle-cap opener/cork remover
- ❑ 1 vegetable scraper
- ❑ 1 Pyrex baking dish, preferably square or rectangular, 4-quart capacity

- ❏ 1 or 2 baking sheets
- ❏ 1 metal roasting pan
- ❏ potholders and/or oven mitts

APPLIANCES
- ❏ A really good blender ("good" means a heavy-duty motor and a glass container. Put this on your Christmas wish list.)
- ❏ A toaster-oven instead of a toaster.

UPGRADE
- ❏ Hand-held mixer
- ❏ Small food-processor/ chopper
- ❏ Non-stick cookware (requires plastic implements instead of metal)
- ❏ Microwave oven
- ❏ Omelet pan

PANTRY
- ❏ Salt
- ❏ White vinegar
- ❏ Cornstarch
- ❏ All-purpose flour
- ❏ Canned chopped tomatoes
- ❏ Canned chicken broth

SPICES
- ❏ Whole peppercorns and pepper grinder
- ❏ Small quantities of dried:
- ❏ Oregano
- ❏ Thyme
- ❏ Basil
- ❏ Cinnamon (ground)
- ❏ Parsley
- ❏ Chicken bouillon, cubes or powder

TOP RÉSUMÉ DON'TS

Your résumé is a paper representation of you. Or rather, it's the person you want to be in the eyes of your employer. That means there are some basic rules to follow when creating your résumé. Specifically, there are several things you don't want to do—assuming you want gainful employment.

❑ **DON'T SEND OUT YOUR RÉSUMÉ WITHOUT HAVING SOMEONE PROOFREAD IT.** Or three someones. Typos are inexcusable on a resume and generally mean you won't even make it to the interview stage.

❑ **DON'T FORGET YOUR CONTACT INFORMATION:** home address, phone and e-mail are all imperative. You never know by what means your future boss will want to contact you. And be sure to update your e-mail address to reflect your newfound maturity—addresses like "hot4ubaby" or "pinkieprettyone" belong to someone who is looking for something other than a job.

❑ **DON'T FORGET TO INCLUDE THE LOCATIONS OF YOUR VARIOUS JOBS.** Employers want to know where you've lived and worked.

❑ **DON'T USE CUTE FONTS.** They don't reflect creativity; they are a sign of immaturity.

❑ **DON'T USE WACKY PAPER.** Sure, it's OK to stand out from the pack by picking a slightly different hue for your résumé. But that one with the paisley? No.

❑ **DON'T INCLUDE PERSONAL INFORMATION.** Your marital status, age, race, family, and hobbies are things you can discuss at the appropriate time; after you discuss your salary.

❏ **DON'T LIE.** You need to back up everything on your resume. If you claim to have visited Paris in college, you need to be prepared to show pictures of your visit. And don't fudge dates to make it look like you've been employed all your life—it will only confuse you during the interview.

❏ **DON'T EXAGGERATE YOUR TALENTS.** If you can speak a little Spanish, don't be tempted to say you are fluent. If you once used InDesign and were confused by it, don't claim it as one of the many computer applications you've mastered.

❏ **DON'T MAKE A JOB SOUND MORE IMPORTANT THAN IT WAS.** Some grads try to jazz up their resume by making a stint at an ice cream shop sound like three months at the United Nations. Employers once had odd jobs, too. Skip the ice cream shop listing, or simply state what it was, without exaggeration.

❏ **DON'T BE MODEST.** If you won an award in college, mention it (assuming it's not something like Most Likely to Get Drunk). If you excelled in sports, mention it. If you traveled for a year abroad, mention it.

THANK-YOU LETTER

*F*irst of all, don't even think about e-mailing a thank-you letter to someone who interviewed you for a job. An e-thanks goes against the advice in just about every etiquette book out there. At the very least, it should be typewritten on quality paper and mailed. Even better, pull out a nice piece of stationary and handwrite your message. Here's a template to give you an idea of what to say.

Date

Name
Title
Organization
Address
City, State, Zip Code

Dear Mr./Ms. Last Name:

I want to thank you for taking time out of your busy schedule to talk to me about the _____ position with your company.

After speaking with you, I do feel that I would be a perfect candidate for this job. As I told you, I have experience in many of the areas that you seek, including _____. Also, after hearing about the responsibilities of the position, I'm very enthusiastic about the possibilities it offers.

Please feel free to contact me at any time if further information is needed. My mobile number is (555) 111-1111.

Thank you again for your time and consideration.

Sincerely,

Your Name

JOB-REJECTION LETTER

*Here's to you being in the position to reject potential employ-
ers due to numerous offers! If this situation comes around,
remember that you shouldn't blow off the people who want to hire
you. Instead, handle your rejection of them by sending a nice
letter confirming that you are seeking a job elsewhere. After all,
you never know how your new job will work out; you might find
yourself working with the people you rejected! Here's a sample
job-rejection letter for your use.*

Date

Name
Title
Street
City, State, Zip Code

Dear Mr./Ms Last Name,

Thank you very much for offering me the position of
_____ with _____. I sincerely appreciate taking
the time to interview me. It was a difficult decision to make, but I
have accepted a position with another company.

Again, thank you for your consideration.

Sincerely,

Your Name

TEN TIPS TO TAKE CHARGE OF YOUR CAREER

*W*ho do you believe is most responsible for guiding your career? Is it your boss, or the company? The answer is you. Master these ten tips and you'll be climbing the corporate ladder in no time.

❑ **FIND A MENTOR:** Do you admire a particular senior executive? Ask him or her to mentor you and show you what it really takes to reach a high level in the company.

❑ **VOLUNTEER FOR OPPORTUNITIES:** Raise your hand willingly and you'll quickly become a valued team player. Pretty soon, executives will be fighting for your services.

❑ **MEET DEADLINES:** Don't let them slip by. Meet your deliverables on time, under budget, and as agreed.

❑ **SUGGEST A NEW PROJECT:** Don't wait for your assignments. Be proactive and suggest new ideas. Become a brainstorming machine and you'll be viewed as innovative.

❑ **BE HELPFUL AND RESOURCEFUL:** Jump in! Lend a hand! Say yes! The more helpful you can be, the more indispensable you'll become to your organization.

❏ **PERFORM AT THE NEXT LEVEL:** Say you're an assistant, eager to get promoted to manager. Start acting like a manager now. Pretty soon your job title will match your effort.

❏ **DEMONSTRATE YOUR EXPERTISE:** Are you a computer whiz? Do you love to present? Reveal your particular strengths and you'll be a high performer in no time.

❏ **GET INVOLVED IN THE INDUSTRY:** Start by joining a professional organization. You'll make connections and master the art of networking.

❏ **RESPOND QUICKLY TO ALL VOICEMAILS AND E-MAILS:** Nobody likes it when their voicemails or e-mails are ignored. Get back to people promptly and you'll earn a reputation as a go-getter.

❏ **ENJOY THE RIDE:** Don't be afraid to smile at work. Your colleagues will perceive you as an approachable, easy-to-work-with partner.

Ten Tips courtesy of Jeff Cohen, principal of Bold Road (www.boldroad.com), a writing, speaking, and consulting company that helps people reach their career, love, and life potential.

TEN TIPS TO TAKE CHARGE OF YOUR JOB INTERVIEW

Say goodbye to clammy hands and rejection letters with these ten tried-and-true tips to help you ace your next interview. Learn these tactics and you'll hear those magic words, "You're hired!"

❏ Dress for success: It's hard to go wrong with a formal suit. At the very least, dress appropriately for the company culture.

❏ Come alive: Passion. Energy. Enthusiasm. If you can't show these emotions in a thirty minute interview, why should the company give you a shot?

❏ Answer the question: There's nothing more frustrating than an interviewee who won't answer the interview questions. Even if the question seems obvious, respond directly.

❏ Give an example: You say you're a project management guru? Don't just say so, back it up with a concrete example from your experience.

❏ Research the company: What does the firm produce? Where is their headquarters? Take the time to know the basics and you'll be ahead of the other candidates.

- ❏ **DON'T BLOW BUBBLES:** Say you're an assistant, eager to get promoted to manager. Start acting like a manager now. Pretty soon your job title will match your effort.

- ❏ **BE HUMBLE:** Arrogance can cancel you out in no time. Check your ego at the door, but don't be afraid to talk with confidence.

- ❏ **ARRIVE ON TIME:** Getting to an interview fashionably late is a sure way to seal your fate. Arrive ahead of schedule and use the extra time to review your notes (see Tip 5).

- ❏ **ASK GREAT QUESTIONS:** Don't ask only about compensation and next steps in the interview process. Wow the interviewer with an insightful, original question.

- ❏ **BRING YOUR RESUME:** Bring extra copies of your resume in case the interviewer wants a fresh one. Never depend on someone else to have what should be your number-one sales tool.

Ten Tips courtesy of Jeff Cohen, principal of Bold Road (www.boldroad.com), a writing, speaking, and consulting company that helps people reach their career, love, and life potential.

CREDITS

Page 2: "Get Smarty," Kim T. Gordon, *Entrepreneur*, October 2004.

Page 4: *www.Wikpedia.org.*

Page 10: Webster's Dictionary.

Page 17: *www.soyouwanna.com.*

Page 20: *www.soyouwanna.com.*

Page 22: *www.EurailPass.com.*

Page 24: U.S. Department of State.

Page 38: "Top 11 Essential Purchases for Your Apartment," Jennifer Lai, About.com.

Page 41: "$100K on a Degree—Now What?" Leslie Haggin Geary, CNN/Money, June 4, 2003.

Page 46: National Association of Colleges and Employers.

Page 54: "Job market looks healthy for 2005 college graduates," Alicia Dorr, *The Columbia Chronicle Online.*

Page 60: Courtesy Princeton University Office of Career Services, " 2005 The Trustees of Princeton University.

Page 69: *www.Forbes.com.*

Page 82: *The Wall Street Journal Top Business Schools 2006*, Ronald J. Alsop with Harris Interactive, Random House, Dow Jones Co. Inc., 2005.

Page 83: *Best 159 Law Schools*, Eric Owens and the staff of the Princeton Review, Random House Inc., 2005, The Princeton Review.

Page 88: Educational Testing Services.

Page 93: "That's Why the Lady Is a Tramp," *The Washington Post*, November 9, 2005.

Page 102: *www.Wikpedia.org.*

Page 107: "Get Smarty," Kim T. Gordon, *Entrepreneur*, October 2004.

Page 108: *www.Evite.com.*

Page 115: "Estimated Age of First Marriage," Current Population Reports, U.S. Census Bureau.

Page 116: "Roberto Cavelli on What's Sexy," *Details*, December 2005.

Page 118: U.S. Census Bureau.

Page 119: "Best Cities for Singles," Lacey Rose and Leah Hoffmann, *www.Forbes.com*, July 25, 2005.

Page 132: "Why Young Americans Are Drowning in Debt," *The Christian Science Monitor* and MSN Money.

Page 139: "Get Smarty," Kim T. Gordon, *Entrepreneur*, October 2004.

Page 156: "Weighing Your Healthcare Choices," *www.ConsumerReports.org.*

SPECIAL THANKS

Thanks to our intrepid "headhunters" for going out to find so many respondents from around the country with interesting advice to share:

Jamie Allen, Chief Headhunter

Andrea Syrtash   Jody Shenn   Nicole Colangelo-
Besha Rodell   Kazz Regelman   Lessin
Carrie Havranek   Ken McCarthy   Shannon Hurd
Connie Farrow   Linda Lincoln   Stacey Shannon
Helen Bond   Natasha Lambropoulos

Thanks, too, to our editorial advisor Anne Kostick. And thanks to our assistant, Miri Greidi, for her yeoman's work at keeping us all organized. The real credit for this book, of course, goes to all the people whose experiences and collective wisdom make up this guide. There are too many of you to thank individually, of course, but you know who you are.

HELP YOUR FRIENDS SURVIVE!

Order extra copies of *How to Survive the Real World,* or one of
our other books.

Please send me:

_____ copies of *How to Survive the Real World,* (@$13.95)

_____ copies of *"You Can Keep the Damn China!"* (@$13.95)

_____ copies of *How to Lose 9,000 Lbs. (or Less)* (@$13.95)

_____ copies of *How to Survive Your Teenager* (@$13.95)

_____ copies of *How to Survive a Move* (@$13.95)

_____ copies of *How to Survive Your Marriage* (@$13.95)

_____ copies of *How to Survive Your Baby's First Year* (@$12.95)

_____ copies of *How to Survive Dating* (@$12.95)

_____ copies of *How to Survive Your Freshman Year* (@$13.95)

Please add $3.00 for shipping and handling for one book, and $1.00 for each
additional book. Georgia residents add 4% sales tax. Kansas residents add
5.3% sales tax. Payment must accompany orders. Please allow three weeks
for delivery.

My check for $_____ is enclosed.

Please charge my __ Visa __ MasterCard __ American Express

Name _____

Organization _____

Address _____

City/State/Zip _____

Phone _____E-mail _____

Credit card # _____

Exp. Date _____Signature _____

Please make checks payable to HUNDREDS OF HEADS BOOKS, LLC

HELP WRITE THE NEXT Hundreds of Heads® SURVIVAL GUIDE!

*Tell us your story about a life experience, and what lesson you learned from it. If we use your story in one of our books, we'll send you a free copy. Use this card or visit **www.hundredsofheads.com**.*

Here's my story/advice on surviving

❏ GETTING INTO COLLEGE (name of college:_____ first choice?_____)

❏ DATING (years dating:_____) (longest relationship:_____)

❏ FINDING A JOB (length of job search: _____)

❏ LOSS OF A LOVED ONE (relationship:_____)

❏ _____ OTHER TOPIC (you pick)

Name: _____City/State: _____

❏ Use my name ❏ Use my initials only ❏ Anonymous

(Note: Your entry in the book may also include city/state and the descriptive information above.)

_____
Signature

How should we contact you *(this will not be published or shared):*

e-mail: _____ other: _____

Please fax to 212-937-2220 or mail to:

HUNDREDS OF HEADS BOOKS, LLC
#230
2221 Peachtree Road, Suite D
Atlanta, Georgia 30309

Your story/advice:

VISIT WWW.HUNDREDSOFHEADS.COM

Do you have something interesting to say about marriage, your in-laws, dieting, holding a job, or one of life's other challenges?

Help humanity—share your story!

 Get published in our next book!

 Find out about the upcoming titles in the HUNDREDS OF HEADS™ survival guide series!

 Read up-to-the-minute advice on many of life's challenges!

 Sign up to become an interviewer for one of the next HUNDREDS OF HEADS® survival guides!

Visit www.hundredsofheads.com today!

ABOUT THE EDITOR

ANDREA SYRTASH is a certified life coach. She studied history and theatre at Queen's University in Ontario, Canada; Middle Eastern studies at the Hebrew University of Jerusalem; and completed a postgraduate degree in broadcast journalism at Ryerson Polytechnic University in Toronto. Although she enjoyed her studies, she learned more about her interests, needs, and talents through the various friendships, romantic relationships and jobs she had after school ended. Andrea has traveled to 28 countries and lived in five cities. She currently resides in her hometown of Toronto, Canada.